MW00377884

BRINGING HOME MORE THAN GROCERIES

You. Are. Not. Alone. Those are the four most powerful words we can offer someone else. We need each other, but sometimes we're not quite sure how to reach out. If you need inspiration to be intentional about doing life with others, this book is for you. Read it. Live it. Enjoy it!

Jill Savage, author of *Better Together: Because You're Not Meant to Mom Alone*

This gift of a book surprised me with several unexpected forms of hospitality. In expanding my view of what it means to gather, Kristin has nourished my own heart while encouraging me to keep what matters most in my changing season as I forego what doesn't. Linger in this book's stories and be encouraged in your own story as you see God's story throughout.

Kristen Strong, author of *Girl Meets Change* and *Back Roads to Belonging*

Kristin invites us into a delightful conversation on the beauty and necessity of hospitality today. She shares stories that remind us hospitality is less about presentation and more about a simple, purposeful invitation into each other's lives. After reading this book, you'll want to be more intentional about finding opportunities to practice hospitality right where you are.

Erin Port, creator of simplepurposefulliving.com

While I love inviting people into my home, my tendencies toward perfectionism and performance often derail my best intentions. What begins as a way to connect with or encourage others turns into a sweaty, stress-fest as I worry more about providing fancy food or shiny clean sinks than I do about offering hugs and authentic friendship. In *Bringing Home More Than Groceries*, Kristin shares her stories—and her friends' stories—of hospitality and the way it can enrich our lives and even grow our faith when we remember why it is we gather in the first place. These stories make me even more determined to step away from Pinterest and step into true hospitality with my people.

Mary Carver, host of The Couch Podcast and author of
Women of Courage: A 40-Day Devotional

Having been the fortunate recipient of Kristin's hospitality, I can say it is generous, uncomplicated, and seems both easy and natural. She's the exact person from whom I want to read a book on hospitality. And this one surely does not disappoint.

Amanda Conquers, writer at amandaconquers.com

BRINGING home & MORE THAN GROCERIES

Stories About Gathering & Nourishing People

kristin hill taylor

Bringing Home More Than Groceries

Author Photo by Dianne Lisette Photography

Cover design and formatting by Mandy Roberson Media

First Edition: 2020

10 9 8 7 6 5 4 3 2 1

To my mom, Cathy Hill, for teaching me the value in feeding people and welcoming them. She always let my friends come over and had plenty of Kool-Aid and Little Debbie snacks to share with them. Now my kids get the blessing of her and her gifts in their lives too.

To my mother-in-law, Peggy Taylor, for welcoming me into the Taylor family long before she really knew me. Now decades later, she still always welcomes me. She's one of my biggest cheerleaders and I've learned so much about loving people from her.

Table of Contents

Season Four: Winter

AN INTRODUCTION

HOSPITALITY GATHERS

I used to be so shy I would avoid people I knew if I saw them from a distance in the grocery store. My mom explained to me more than once that I came across rude, but mustering the courage to make small talk seemed so scary.

Then I grew up and decided to study journalism in college. Having a bachelor's degree from Murray State University in Murray, Ky., a place I now call home, didn't make me a journalist, but it helped. After a couple short-term jobs, I settled in the newsroom at the *Murray Ledger & Times*, regularly asking a bunch of questions of university presidents, state senators, city councilmen, judges, policemen and -women, and people who turned out to be neighbors with whom I'd now make small talk when I saw them while I grocery shopped in Kroger.

Turns out I wasn't shy anymore.

Then I became a mom. Just four-and-a-half months into motherhood, I made the decision to stay at home with my daughter, leaving a career I thought I would juggle with my new role. I didn't stop writing or asking questions, though. Now I write in the cracks of my day, jotting down notes in my phone. I ask questions as I mother and while I catch up with friends over lunch. Each trip through the aisles of the grocery store inspired me. Each time we invited people over for dinner around our table taught me something about myself and my community. Each time someone invites me into their house, I know a deeper belonging.

Now, the mother of three children—Cate, Ben, and Rachel— who you'll learn much about in the coming pages, I have learned life is best shared. Togetherness often involves preparing so we can share a meal and linger on the porch, having a freezer full of Popsicles and ice cream sandwiches to treat my pool guests, and accepting invitations into others' lives.

Come with me, into the aisles of Kroger—the chain grocery store in La Grange, Ky., where my mom took me as a child that also has a similar store in Murray, Ky., where I now go at least once a week. And even if you aren't familiar with Kroger, come along, thinking of the Publix, Target, or Walmart that you know so well.

Come with me, into my kitchen, which is always open and serves as a gathering place for my people—the ones who live here and the ones who don't. I'll tell you to help yourself to a drink from our extra fridge in the laundry room or let you make your own coffee.

Come with me, onto my porch. This is my favorite place to host and linger and live. You can see your kids jumping on the trampoline or swimming in the pool from here. There are lights if we want to stay out past dark. The best days are when my family can eat three meals and countless snacks all in one day out there. Yes, it's easier to clean up the porch, but it's also freer living for my soul.

You'll meet some of my dearest friends along the way as I share real-life stories and what I've learned from doing life together. Plus, at the end of each chapter, you'll meet a friend who has a story of her own to share. These stories come from real-life friends. We've shared meals and so many moments. I couldn't imagine a hospitality book without other voices because of the simplest lesson of all: We're better together.

When I grocery shop, I bring home more than bags of cheese, fruit, eggs, milk, and ice cream. Along with the bags, my heart also is filled life lessons, preparations for meals that create bonds that truly sustain me, and glimpses of my children as they become who they're created to be.

Sometimes hospitality is flinging the doors to your home and life wide open for others to enter. Other times it means accepting invitations elsewhere because God has something for you there. Like everything in life, hospitality has seasons. What we do, what we eat, what's on sale at the grocery, where we go, who comes with us all vary depending on circumstances and seasons—and through it all hospitality is love in action.

Spring

Seasons changed, and we changed with them. Every day became its own kind of spring, good things growing from low places, belonging to everyone, teaching us to stick our necks out, take a risk, and bloom in spite of struggle.

Shannan Martin in *The Ministry of Ordinary Places*

HOSPITALITY BEGINS

My mom usually let us get a candy bar at Kroger's check-out aisle. These candy bars were threatened if we didn't behave ourselves as she weaved the cart through the aisles.

I had no idea at the time, but I now understand that hauling three kids who were born within four-and-a-half years to the grocery after school or on the weekend was a big deal. She worked full time teaching fifth-graders about the Revolutionary War and other subjects, provided taxi service to all our activities in a maroon Ford Escort and then later a red Ford Aerostar minivan, and never let us go hungry or without whatever else we desired. I seriously don't remember my mom complaining—about grocery shopping with kids in tow, about us inviting our friends over and then offering them Fritos and Kool-Aid, or about us adding another thing to the calendar. As a mom now, I know she must have been tired—and I don't even have a full-time job outside of the house.

My mom would still do anything for us—me, my sister, my brother, our spouses, and the eight grandchildren. Of course, now she likes to give the grandkids candy bars or whatever else she finds at Sam's that makes her think of them.

Truthfully, even as a kid, I didn't mind going to the grocery. What I did mind was running into people I knew. My shy personality prompted me to play a hide-and-seek game only I knew I was playing, ducking in the next aisle when I saw someone I knew. It's not because I didn't like them, but I worried that they wouldn't recognize me or notice me and I'd have to strike up an awkward conversation.

My mom will tell you stories about me hanging onto her leg—literally—like I thought she could shield me from the world. I really did think she would and could and should protect me. I don't really know when I grew out of the shyness, but it was one step at a time, beginning as I found my voice through writing in high school and college. Regardless, I'm thankful I don't usually want to cling to my mom's leg now that I'm a grown-up girl with kids of my own.

Even so, the people who knew me when I probably tried to hide from them haven't forgotten. When I was 28 years old, some friends threw me a baby shower in honor of my newborn daughter Cate. My friends and relatives took turns sharing a memory. This kind of thing still makes me nervous. Maybe that's just the shyness slipping back into existence. When it was my mom's turn at this baby shower, she reminisced about my shy days. I think she still likes to talk about it, but that's okay because she always eventually gets around to how I've grown up and grown out of that tendency.

"Kristin was so shy as a kid. She didn't speak to people and hung on my leg. But then she grew up and become a journalist. Can you believe she called people who didn't want to talk to her?"

Indeed, I'm not shy anymore. At least not like that little-girl shy. I'd still rather text than make a phone call. I'm raising a girl who is so much like me, but I'm thankful she's not as shy as me. When Cate was just learning to talk, she would talk to anyone, including strangers at the grocery store. Now that she's entering her teenage years, she's a little more selective with whom she strikes up in conversation, but once she gets going, her words come fast, blend together, and contain so many details. Sometimes I have to ask her to slow down so I can understand her.

The moral of the story is sometimes people will surprise you. My mom finds joy in me gaining enough confidence to move beyond her leg and be the reporter on the other end of the phone.

So journalist-turned-momma it is.

These days I squeeze in trips to the grocery between other errands, stock up on snacks for my kids' friends, and drive my own momma taxi service. I've also taught my kids their role in this whole grocery shopping scenario. Even if I pick up groceries while they're at school, it's usually their job to haul in all the sacks. Hey, it's just tradition around here.

Mom and I had a routine once we got home from the grocery. I'd carry some bags in and then start putting the groceries away as Mom continued to carry in the bags and recruited my younger brother and sister to help. I'd organize boxes on their proper shelves, stack frozen items in just a way that everything would fit, and put the Kool-Aid packets in the canister next to the sugar and flour (What? Not everyone had a canister for sugary drink mixes?). I still want everything in the pantry and fridge where it belongs, so I let my kids carry in the bags while I put away all the items.

Mom frequently went grocery shopping, probably in part because of all the people she let me invite over. We lived in a horse-shoe-shaped neighborhood where, during some of my favorite years, one best friend lived diagonally behind me and my other best friend lived right next door facing the same cul-de-sac as our house. One winter Elizabeth and I killed a path of grass through the neighbor's yard that separated our two houses. Of course, we didn't realize it until the spring when most of the grass sprouted green. Katie and I knew how many steps it was from her bedroom door to mine. We played flashlight tag with the boys who hung out at Rob's house on the other side of the horseshoe. And, of course, my mom would have a pantry of snacks available to whoever ended up in our kitchen.

On Schureck Court in Buckner, Kentucky, is where I learned about hospitality—although it would be many years before I learned this term and realized not everyone embraces it. It's just the life I knew, thanks to my mom. In so many ways, my husband's childhood was different than mine, but being the house where friends gathered happened for him too. So that's the life we continue to live, starting with our immediate family of five and circling outward as we connect with others.

Some things never change as we grow up and settle into our own lives. I'm thankful I don't usually play secret games of hide-and-seek, but I do hope I'm raising kids who will always want to help carry the load—whether that's canned goods or whatever else life throws our way. I may even get them a candy bar next time we're at Kroger.

STORY OF SHARED LIFE
KATIE KERNS

It happened when I was twenty-three years old. Maybe it had been creeping up on me since childhood when I found an unhealthy amount of pride in organizing stuffed animals on my bed, but this was the moment that it really stuck. The moment that I heard the lie: Hospitality is equivalent to perfection.

Married for a little over a week, my new husband and I hitched up a U-Haul trailer behind his 1994 Honda station wagon, said goodbye to friends and family, and drove the 1,000-plus miles to New England to start our life together. We spent hours cleaning, organizing, hanging pictures, and scooting our particleboard furniture around to make the most out of a 500-square-foot brownstone apartment, which was situated between Fenway Park and Boston University, where Brad was starting on his master's degree in trombone. Our first guests walked through the door into our very small space, and while I don't remember the words verbatim, I'm certain it was something innocuous and obligatory like, "How cute!"

That's all it took. That was the moment. I was plummeted into the depths of idolizing domestic excellence and mistaking that for true, warm hospitality. No matter where we lived, it was the same. Parents coming over for dinner? Friends visiting from out of town? Potential UPS delivery where the guy might see into the foyer through my front door? It had to have been incredible to watch, honestly. I would instantly break out into a panicked sweat and begin the fevered routine: "Dust. Vacuum. Mop. Straighten up books on the bookshelves. Wipe down kitchen. Wash (or hide) dirty dishes. Take out the trash. Clean the bathrooms. Scrub things that literally no one will see. Make beds. Fluff pillows. Light candles. Throw everything that doesn't have a precise place into a basket and shove the basket into a corner. Fold a cute blanket and place it perfectly over the couch, like I casually tossed it there. Sweep the porch. Should I run to Kroger to get bananas to put in the wooden fruit bowl? Oh, no. Where is my wooden fruit bowl?!"

It was great fun, obviously. Not exhausting whatsoever. And in those first years of married life, I had so many gentle opportunities from God to see the truth of hospitality—having a dog meant fur on everything, working full-time meant less time to fixate on the details, owning a home meant more space to manage, having a baby meant things were going to be out of place, having another baby meant EVERYTHING was going to be out of place. But still I tried. I labored over things that weren't bringing our friends and family comfort when they were with me. If anything, I'm sure they could sense my stress and wondered why I was throwing coasters at them for their drinks instead of just curling up and spending time with them. I had moments of clarity, of course, but no lasting peace in this area of my life. I was unable to navigate the waters of hospitality without feeling like I was drowning.

Then when I was thirty-one, a surprising life-preserver was tossed to me in the form of Brad's new job. He landed the position at the University of Kentucky as the professor of trombone. This meant college students. Lots and lots of college students. Do you know what college students don't care about? A messy house. Do you know what they do care about? A fridge they can open to find their favorite sodas. A pantry they know is always stocked with snacks. Dogs that cuddle up next to them on a comfortable couch. Invitations to play LEGOs with two elementary school boys who hang on every word and think every joke is funny. A big hug when they walk in, and a safe place they can rest and forget about exams, recitals, concerts, and college drama for a couple of hours. I suddenly found myself living in a home that could be invaded by hordes of almost-adults at a moment's notice. Almost-adults who I love with all my heart. Some of these are now full-grown adults and dear friends who know they don't have to call before they drop by for a visit.

God healed my heart and adjusted my motives in the sweetest way through Brad's college students, and that's when my understanding of hospitality finally began. I no longer believe a house that looks perfect means that it's full of love. Quite the opposite now. And my routine when I know someone is going to drop by? I just open the door.

Katie Kerns *is a wife, mom of two boys, and teacher. She loves God, her family and friends, iced coffee, singing Disney songs, petting dogs, and hugging.*

HOSPITALITY TEACHES

Running errands is often more fun when someone else is along for the ride—even when that someone else is a kid.

I remember being so glad to be a mom when I hauled Cate around while I tried to maintain my productive ways. I probably should have shifted my mindset of what productivity was really necessary and how I defined a successful day long before I did. But Cate was fun to have along, and she was and still is an easy kid. I watch her love life and realize that's part of the child-like faith Jesus encourages us adults to have. She trusts I'll take care of her, meet her physical and emotional needs, and even bless her sometimes beyond what is required. Ben and Rachel have added even more of that dynamic to my everyday life, and managing three kids is emotionally and logistically more challenging for me. In addition, their personalities aren't quite as easy for me to parent, while Cate is so much like me so I naturally understand her. Plus, regardless of her age, running errands doesn't dampen her spirit. Now, at twelve years old, she actually enjoys shopping.

When Cate was not walking or talking yet, the grocery store seemed to be among her favorite stops. She liked to look at the many colors lining the shelves, babbling and pointing as we walked methodically from one aisle to the next. She made friends with whomever we passed, especially other little kids and the older women who loved on her with their sweet words. And we had little games we played at Kroger. Sometimes I counted—"one, two, three ..."—and then walked really fast down the aisle. Other times I sang, "Peanut, peanut butter, JELLY!" (The condiment aisle always prompted that song.)

The baggers loved her too. She always tried to reach out and help them. Her big, brown eyes followed their every movement, first as they loaded the yogurt and applesauce into plastic bags and then as they strategically loaded it all back into the cart. Sometimes we were in a cashier named Diego's check-out lane and he told her about his cousin Dora. Cate just smiled and babbled about something else, even though she was too young to have any idea what he was talking about. She later loved Dora and quickly made the connection.

We usually made another playful run to our car, which was conveniently parked next to a cart corral. I unloaded Cate from her cushy cart seat—thanks to the Floppy Seat that cushioned and prevented her little mouth from chewing on the public shopping cart—and then packed the trunk.

Then we'd do it again the next week. Each trip marked her physical and mental growth. Once she started walking, we'd walk into Kroger holding hands and talk about the seasonal displays of lawn chairs, pumpkins, or Christmas trees. For a couple of years, Cate got the life of luxury being pushed around by momma once we were inside the store.

Then one day when Cate was almost two, she noticed a green and yellow car attached to the front of a shopping cart. With great enthusiasm, she said, "I drive. I drive." Okay, sure. How bad could it be? She got in and off we went . . . right into the Granny Smith apple display. Apparently momma's driving needed a little more practice. Once I got back on course, I ran her right into the standing dispenser of produce bags, then I got the entire stand stuck on the cart.

Maybe letting Cate "drive" wasn't a good idea because it was really complicating my driving! In effort to keep people from watching me run into more things (because even as an adult I despise being the center of attention), I figured out that if I pushed down on the handle bar while I pushed the car forward, I could offset her weight in the front. I noticed the wheels closest to me weren't touching because there wasn't much in the basket yet. So, I solved the problem, kept the wheels on the ground, and proceeded forward in a much safer fashion.

Cate obviously was pleased with the outing because I lost count of how many times she said: "I driving. I driving." Yes, you drove like a pro through that store—and momma was doing a better job too.

I quieted the thoughts of people telling me my baby wouldn't be a baby for long. I quickly moved on from thinking about how she'll be 16—and really driving!—before I knew it. And I concentrated on making sure my girl didn't get out of her car cart while the bagger asked if I want the groceries loaded back into the same cart. Oh, yes, we're pros now, and I'm guessing there's never ever going to be any going back to a regular cart with this kid.

The weekly trips to the store continued and so did the toddler driving when I become a mom to a second child. As my family grew, so did the armfuls of stuff that I brought into the store with me. I entered Kroger armed with the diaper bag and a reusable bag, which was filled with other reusable bags, hanging on my shoulder; Ben in the car seat carrier on the bend of my right arm; and Cate, who usually had a purse, plastic cell phone, or some other accessory, holding my left hand. And, strangely enough, I didn't mind grocery shopping like this.

Thankfully, those car carts also accommodated my second child.

I remember one shopping trip, when my high-maintenance baby Ben, who was about four months old, was crying. Really, I should probably say he was screaming. As was the case much of his babyhood, I wasn't sure what was wrong or how to soothe him. And let me tell you: a crying/screaming baby sure attracts comments.

"Is that you making all that noise?" someone I knew said as she looked right at me. "Um, no, not me." Then I faked a smile.

Strangers joined the moment: "Oh, now, he's not happy." Um, you think?

"I remember those days," another stranger said. Then she smiled, like she really wanted to tell me it was going to be okay. I smiled back, wanting to say I've had louder, more intense moments from one or both of my children.

Ben cried for a few more aisles. Then he gave into contentment for the last portion of the grocery shopping trip, which included Cate's request for a bathroom break. Of course. She loved public bathrooms and she hadn't been potty-trained long enough for me to deny her request.

And, yes, more comments came as I carried my baby in his carrier on one arm and held my toddler's hand while walking into the store bathroom: "You'll miss these days. You don't think you will. But you will." I did try to realize I'd miss this. Probably not so much the group trip to the Kroger bathroom in the middle of the grocery shopping experience, but I was sure I'd miss the little people who needed me and wanted me and thought I was the best thing since the cheese cubes I let them pick out in the dairy section. But we welcomed our third baby when the other two kids were eight and almost six years old, so I prolonged the "you're going to miss this" thing. I also started leaving the reusable bags at home because I didn't need one more thing to hold.

After the bathroom, we headed to the check-out line, which was at least six people deep. Cate struck up a conversation with a grandfatherly farmer, who has a granddaughter "about her age," he told us. Turns out, the granddaughter was a year older, liked to wear pink, had a special bond with his farm animals, and liked to eat white beans, fried cornbread, and cabbage. Somehow the grandfatherly farmer and I didn't discuss why there were only two check-out lanes open, one of which was the Express Lane, for which he qualified with his two-liter of Coke, ice cream, and cabbage, or why he chose to stand in the long line with his obviously less than fifteen items.

I'm glad life doesn't have an Express Line. Life may be chaotic and unpredictable, but it is these moments, these people, all these many words, this time. And I did realize it's not going to be like this forever—or even next week.

In what seemed like the next week, my three-year-old girl decided it was time to move from the car cart to the miniature grocery cart that threatens mommas' ankles everywhere.

Cate hit my heels with her cart almost immediately and I remembered the look my mom would give me when I walked too closely behind her and literally stepped on her feet. She didn't want to be mad but being tripped up is never fun. I'm certain I gave Cate the same look. And then I told her to stay close but to watch where she was going. Oh, she watched, that's for sure. And she wanted to put everything in her cart as she touched lots of things on shelves. None of this was surprising, especially because this was the first time she had walked in Kroger. Ah, freedom—and with a toddler-sized cart. But we didn't need the pourable Bisquick mix.

Lesson time: I explained that momma had a list and that wasn't on it. She seemed to understand, especially when I let her pick the items we did need off the shelves. The only non-list item that made it into her cart was a package of mini marshmallows. And, hey, she asked nicely. At one point, I stopped in the canned vegetable aisle to evaluate my list. I caught a glimpse of Cate pretending she had a list in one hand and a pen in the other. Apparently, she was marking off "marshmallows."

We filled her little cart and my big cart. Thankfully, Ben didn't scream this time. The bagger loaded groceries back into both of our carts—and somehow they didn't all fit so we added a third overflow cart to the mix. We all headed to the parking lot, where I got the kids buckled in, the groceries loaded, and then handed the kids that bag of marshmallows. I took a deep breath and congratulated myself on a successful outing.

Grocery shopping isn't a one-time affair, though. My first-born craves routine like I do. Do something once, and she assumes it has to happen that way every single time. With little kids then and big kids now, I have to remind myself it's about more than going through the motions.

When she was three, Cate had blind faith when she followed me up and down the aisles while pushing her miniature shopping cart. She liked feeling in control. And, of course, she wanted to do it all herself—push the cart, add the strawberries and lettuce to the cart, pick the Honey Nut Cheerios off the shelf, unload the groceries at the check-out lane, and then push her cart with the now-bagged groceries to the minivan.

Even then I knew I wanted to remember her faith, how she just followed me, sometimes not even looking as she turned the corner, barely missing the end-of-the-aisle display of Juicy Juice. She went where I went. She knew which foods I'd choose off the shelves. She got distracted from what was in front of her when she turned her head around to continue talking to the lady we just passed. So, of course, I rattled off cart-driving instructions: "Honey, you have to watch where you're going. Put your head up. And follow me."

Then I realized what I said. I asked her to trust me, yet also watch where she was going. My heart swelled when I saw the bigger picture that time because I could hear my heavenly Father say something similar to me: "Kristin, watch where you're going. Keep your head up because I'm with you. Follow me all your days."

Now, of course, I tell Cate that Ben and Rachel are watching her and following her lead. (No wonder first-borns are the way we are.) She doesn't always believe me because she doesn't trust love from her little brother who sometimes looks like pestering and admiration from her little sister who usually demands much. On repeat around here: We're all on the same team.

There was a time at Kroger when Cate and Ben were happy to be on the same team.

It had been a while since I had them both along for grocery shopping because my girl grew up and became a kindergartner.

"Can I push a little cart?" my 3-year-old Ben piped up from the middle row in the minivan.

"Yeah, do we both get to push little carts?" kindergartner Cate said from the row behind her brother.

You know, honestly, I hadn't thought about this quandary. Ben had started pushing the little cart while she was in school.

I conditioned my response with, "if there are two." Yes, I secretly hoped there wouldn't be two kid-sized carts available, but, of course, two carts were awaiting my kids' fingers this one March afternoon.

I walked into the produce section with Cate pushing her cart just behind my heels. Ben was pushing at an equally quick pace, just behind his sister's heels. He was so close we weren't even to the bananas when she shouted, "Mom, he just hit my heels with his cart."

My eyes looked at her and said enough. Then I followed that up with, "Now you know why I tell you to be careful and watch where you're going." Sometimes reality is the best teacher and team builder.

These little moments of motherhood are ones I cherished then and look back with fondness, even now as those two have moved on into later elementary and middle schools. I hope they learned something too.

STORY OF SHARED LIFE
KAYLA SLACK

I'm sure you could take a hospitality class that would teach you how to set the perfect table, send out the perfect invites, and try to be your most perfect self. I fully believe no class will teach you like real-life experiences will. I did not understand hospitality until someone decided to invite me in. Sometimes the simple act of someone being hospitable teaches you how to be hospitable too.

My life completely changed when my husband and I had kids. My life became focused on them. Of course, we are called to care for and nurture our children. My husband and children are supposed to be my priority and I love that they are. However, I let all other parts of me fall aside. They became my all unintentionally and I let everything else go in my life. I forgot what true friendship was like. I forgot that I love community and connection.

Thankfully I met someone who understood connection. Upon my first interaction with her I loved how she just welcomed in all the people around her. Not just into her surroundings but into her heart. She had a way of making a place feel safe for anyone around her. She made me feel this way too and I had just met her. She had a way about her that created gatherings out of people who didn't know each other, making them all feel like they belong together.

I've been to gatherings all my life. Family reunions, birthday parties, church potlucks, you name it. Of course, we all had a good time, but they felt scheduled and almost fake. My friend taught me it is okay to come as you are. Gift or no gift. Food or no food. She taught me I don't have to bring a thing but that I'm welcome and have a place with her and her people.

Meeting this friend and seeing how she welcomed in so many totally changed my view on hospitality. I never thought to allow friends to come over while my house was a mess. I always thought I had to have the good plates out and food available. I never thought to gather a group of people who didn't know each other together. It isn't about the plates. It isn't about the food. It isn't about knowing everyone in the room.

Hospitality is not the hotel-like approach where things are perfectly manicured in a way that feels cold and distant. The real version of hospitality is where someone invites you to be the full version of yourself with them, where a place is made for you to feel open bringing your entire life into their life, the messy and fun and painful parts. Hospitality is about friendship and just being together, regardless of the food or activities (even though those are great too). I'm thankful I had someone who could teach me what hospitality really means. She taught me it is about true friendship and she taught me how to be a friend.

Kayla Slack *is a wife, mama of two, and home health nurse who finds joy in Jesus and her life with her family.*

HOSPITALITY HEALS

Less than eighteen hours after my seven-year-old Ben sustained second-degree burns to his face and hands, I found myself in a grocery store. It wasn't my usual one. We were two hours from home because Ben had been admitted to the burn unit at Vanderbilt Medical Center.

I walked into a Publix with my two girls, the oldest of whom was doing a fabulous job holding us together even though she wasn't quite ten years old. I carried my toddler without shoes because I didn't have the energy or the time to put her shoes back on . . . again.

We were at the grocery store because we wanted some breakfast after eating pretzels and crackers from the hotel for a late dinner the night before. The girls and I had stayed at a hotel because at 10 o'clock that night Ben was still hanging out in an emergency room bed, and I knew some of us had to get sleep if we were going to walk through these circumstances together. Of course, sleep didn't come easy because I don't like my family to be separated under the best circumstances. Plus, I was sharing a hotel bed with my then-eighteen-month-old girl who had never slept in a bed that didn't contain her. And, yes, her instinct was to jump.

I stood there in Publix recounting what had happened the day before and simultaneously thinking about the many beach vacations in my past. I might have been in Nashville, Tennessee, but I was far enough south to be in the grocery store that reminded me of the grocery runs to fill the Florida condo refrigerator when I was a child. Meanwhile, my mind was spinning and full of the constant replay stream of hearing Ben scream on the other side of the woods while I was lying in a hammock reading a book on the Sunday afternoon to start spring break.

We didn't know how long Ben would be at the hospital or how long our toddler would endure the stroller and its buckles. So I bought bananas, squeezy pouches of applesauce, fruit snacks, and candy. Take me out of my usual element and I will find comfort in familiar road trip food.

I left the grocery store that morning with a bag full of distractions for us and then headed for my boy, who was then and still is one of the bravest people I know. I walked into the hospital room to see my boy with his oh-so-swollen and darkened face eating scrambled eggs and French toast. He didn't need my store-bought breakfast after all.

Even so, I was thankful for my momma instincts again. Ben and Greg were out of sight when I heard Ben scream the afternoon before. I knew something was wrong when I heard my boy, so I rushed through the house, grabbed my rain boots and ran through the forest to the guys and the burn pile. I saw Greg spraying Ben with water. Apparently, the brush pile they'd intentionally lit on fire unintentionally flared up as Ben was standing up from having been leaned over to light it.

As soon as they told me what happened, I knew we needed to go to the emergency room. We didn't see evidence of burns yet, but Ben was clearly in pain. We walked quickly back to the house, changed Ben out of his wet clothes, got more comfortable shoes for me, put more water on his hands, and took off for the local emergency room, which is about fifteen minutes away.

Long story short: Ben was transferred to Vanderbilt Medical Center, where he spent two nights in the burn unit being treated for second-degree burns on his hands and face.

I remember looking at Ben that morning eating his breakfast less than twenty-four hours after the accident, and his face was so swollen his left eye could barely open. The doctors and nurses at Vanderbilt's burn unit kept telling us to give his skin two weeks to heal. In a single moment, looking at my boy who didn't look like himself, two weeks seemed so far away yet like not enough time for his wounds to heal and his new skin to grow. But they were right. It's not that I doubted them; they're experts. But I couldn't see very well beyond that single moment.

There's a lot I could tell you about these circumstances and what they did for our family. Obviously, Ben suffered pain, but the emotions were all over the place for all of us. We were scared and worried and relieved and thankful. Our family of five was changed —in good ways—because trauma offers perspective.

During that time our community of people surrounded us with prayers, encouragement, meals, supplies, medical advice, and their presence. In this experience, community was a broad circle including our closest friends, acquaintances who wanted to help, school friends, church friends, Facebook friends who get peeks in our lives.

I watched my son's face and hands grow new skin quicker than I ever thought possible. I shed tears because seeing my boy uncomfortable was hard and caring for him involved a whole new skill set for me that was overwhelming. But even more powerful than all of that was how we were overwhelmed with the love and prayers. When I told Ben how hundreds of people were praying for him, he was amazed. Truly, I was too—not because I doubt God or my friends but because coming alongside trauma can be hard.

At the time, I got so many texts that offered prayers and love. People asked what they could do with genuine kindness. Friends showed up at my house with Dilly Bars and a prayer spoken aloud over my boy, fasted for a day to focus on praying for us, gave of their time to help Ben with his stretches that he didn't always want to do for his parents, brought meals and treats, and ran my errands.

Around the same time, I read Lisa-Jo Baker's book called *Never Unfriended* and our reality brought her words to life for me: "Being willing to be a neighbor in the heart sense of the word is being willing to connect with the people who God puts in our path. It's doing life together, especially the hard parts. It's choosing friendship on purpose."[1]

Some of our neighbors showed up at our house, where Ben doesn't usually wear a shirt and had a Vaseline-like medicine all over his face. Others showed up in texts and on Voxer. Some sent love through the postal service. Regardless of where they were, I was grateful they were my neighbors during the experience. Ben is 100 percent extroverted and asked if people were coming to visit before we left the hospital. I'm glad they showed up because that's what helped him to get up and move his hands. He played the Wii with almost everyone who walked in our house and forgot that his hands were wrapped in gauze.

I let a hairdresser friend pick up Cate from school and cut her hair in my kitchen when they got here. I needed help encouraging Ben to do his hand and face exercises, so I reached out to a friend from church who does physical therapy with nursing home patients and said yes to a friend from school who used to do rehab work with stroke and cancer patients. I said yes to another church friend who organized a Meal Train and the friends who signed up to bring us food. Another friend got to be Ben's home health nurse. Other friends sent muffins and candy and cards. And then many stayed to pray and play with my boy.

Often hospitality is about being available and willing. Hospitality is showing up, living generously, accepting help, offering help, and sharing your front porch. "Hospitality" and "hospital" have the same word origin, so no wonder hospitality heals. Yes, welcoming someone to your table is an invitation to something more than dinner. In *Outlive Your Life*, author and pastor Max Lucado describes how our hospitality can be someone else's hospital: "Something holy happens around a dinner table that will never happen in a sanctuary. In a church auditorium you see the backs of heads. Around the table you see the expressions on faces. In the auditorium one person speaks; around the table everyone has a voice. Church services are on a clock. Around the table there is time to talk. Hospitality opens the door to uncommon community. … Your hospitality can be their hospital."[2]

I love that we found a different kind of hospital happening in our own home after we left the actual hospital. This is what friendship is about. It helps us heal from trauma and reminds us that even the scary stories can have beauty. It was also a living example of what Paul wrote to the Romans (and ultimately us) about hospitality: "Contribute to the needs of the saints and seek to show hospitality" (Romans 12:13). In fact, "seek to show hospitality" can also mean "practice hospitality," based on the original language described in

Blue Letter Bible.[3] This is in the passage that begins: "Let love be genuine ..." (Romans 12:9). Meeting needs and showing hospitality are love. Sometimes we just show up for one another as we're all trying to figure out life together.

Ben was cleared to go back to school after ten days and had brand-new skin within two weeks—just like the doctors said. In the big picture, his physical healing happened quickly. Even so, it was a hard story for us to live, but, by God's grace, we didn't have to do it alone.

Hospitality is continuing to show up for others and letting people show up for you. Again, Lisa-Jo Baker is wise on this topic: "But we just kept showing up. . . Because when you tell your stories, you start to recognize yourself in the stories of others. You start to discover that you are both, in fact, inside a shared story."[4]

The characters and circumstances aren't always the same, but the common threads of exhaustion, fear, joy, and hope matter. Those and others were my emotions as my boy healed. Yet we welcomed people into our real life—when the floor wasn't swept, most of us weren't showered, and exhaustion was our close companion. That open door helped us all heal.

STORY OF SHARED LIFE
SARAH GOODRICH

It was late March of 2003 when I received a three-page, hand-written letter in the mail from my big brother, Chris. For the entirety of the three pages, Chris was trying to convince me to move from my apartment in Lexington, Kentucky, to the home he shared with his wife and three children in Carmel, Indiana. By the end of August of that year, I had moved in with Chris, Joy, Cailin (five years old), Jaron (three), and Bethany (seven months).

Chris and Joy had not spent a great deal of time and energy convincing me to move in with them because I was going to be a fun houseguest. They pursued me because I was in the middle of a major depression. I had lost a lot of sleep, a lot of weight, a lot of tears, and a lot of maddening hours wondering what in the world was wrong with me. I had nothing about which to be depressed. I loved my family, my job, my roommate, and my circle of friends. But as many sufferers of depression know, sometimes there just is not an identifiable reason, and that made me feel even worse. After I got his letter, I sobbed on the phone to Chris, "I can't move in with you! I'll cry all the time." He said, "That's okay." At a time when I was broken, they extended to me a very selfless and generous hospitality.

I do not remember a lot of the daily details of what turned into nearly four years of living with Chris and Joy, but the memories that stand out will, I'm certain, stay with me forever. As soon as I arrived, they told me that I could control my level of interaction with them. If I wanted to be alone in my room, that was perfectly acceptable. If I wanted to spend time with the family, they would welcome me with open arms. I never paid them one cent. No rent, no utilities, no grocery money, and never did I pay for myself when we went out to eat together. Chris and Joy insisted that I be in their Christmas photos. We had many long talks. In all the time I lived with them, I do not remember a single, solitary time in which there was any kind of argument or hard feelings. I worked retail, and I remember frequently coming home in the middle of the night and making a snack. I do not remember washing my dishes. My baby niece went through a phase of calling me and her mother, "Mama." If dirty midnight dishes and your baby calling another woman Mama don't make you want to kick out your houseguest, I don't know what will.

I left their house in May 2007. I'm not sure anything but true love could have torn me away. The move was necessary to start my job back in Kentucky, where my fiancé, Nathan, was in law school. In September of that year, Nathan and I got married. Halfway through our walk down the aisle, Chris joined me and Dad. Joy and my nieces were beaming, beautiful members of our wedding party. They were big parts of our wedding because I don't think the wedding would have happened if Chris and Joy had not allowed themselves to be used by God in extravagant hospitality. I arrived to them broken, and I left them a completely different person, healed.

Sarah Goodrich lives in Frankfort, Kentucky, with her husband and four children.

HOSPITALITY ADVENTURES

A year before Ben was burned, after church and lunch on Easter 2016, my family of five explored the thirty-three acres we had recently purchased. A renovation was almost underway and we wouldn't move for a few more months, but Greg reached out his arm and took our picture in front of our new-to-us house. For me, that moment held so much hope of what was to come as we prepared for our new country living adventure together.

A couple weeks after Ben was burned, I made my family assemble in similar pose before we went to the breakfast potluck before our church service. It was Easter again and time was nudging me to pause and remember.

I was a little nervous about moving to the country, where friends and stores aren't quite as convenient. "Living out of town" in small-town lingo meant we were fifteen minutes away instead of three. I grew up in a subdivision with one entrance where I befriended certain neighbors and knew plenty about the other ones. I spent four years of college living in a dorm with my best friends in my room, through the shared bathroom, down the hall, or no farther than across campus. After college, I lived in apartments in Kentucky's two largest cities. Even in small-town Murray, I lived in two different houses off the busiest four-lane where I could walk to the park, restaurants, and stores.

I wasn't sure what a change to country scenery would do for our social life, but the move felt right. We're still here in a house surrounded by woods and creeks. And, guess what, friends have shown up for small group meetings, game nights filled with roasted potatoes and Settlers of Catan, lunches with chicken salad and other adoptive moms.

Rachel learned to climb stairs before we moved to the country and how I was grateful for a single-level home for my fearless girl to explore. She walked in the living room four months after we moved in and hasn't stopped getting into things yet. She runs in the wide-open fields and loves riding through our woods and down the logging road in our Kawasaki mule.

Four years after we moved, we spent much time at home during the worldwide coronavirus epidemic. I loved my days at home, where I could drown out the chaos of the world and rest in peace at the creeks and walks down tree-lined paths. When I ventured to town to get groceries, I brought anxiety home with me. Our world shifted that spring and I'm thankful our country home calmed my heart, even though we did miss opening our doors to others during that time.

Maybe a move eight miles outside a small town doesn't seem significant, but for me it has been. I learned dreams change and God binds together his people. I know God has me where he has me for reasons I've experienced deeply and ones I don't even know about yet.

We hosted a bonfire with friends from church one evening when the days were growing shorter. This is something we'd wanted to do for a long time, so we were glad to gather some branches and sticks, stock up on s'mores fixings, and make sure our flashlights had batteries. The night included pots of chili inside, so people were going back and forth, in and out all evening. But what I'll remember is our worship leader bringing what usually happens in front of the congregation in our church building to us on hay bales around a fire that had to be poked to remain aglow. He led us in singing a song that seemed to capture the moment for me:

"Lord, prepare me to be a sanctuary

Pure and holy, tried and true

With thanksgiving, I'll be a living

Sanctuary for you"[5]

Sanctuary means a "place of safety or refuge." That's exactly what country living had become for me. That's what the hospitality that happened here did for my soul that day and so many others.

We didn't live here in the spring we bought this property, but we stopped by to check on things periodically. Living here when the grass and trees become greener brings healing and adventures. Now

I know where the daffodils pop up, often in February, and I wonder if they'll really survive March. Somehow they do.

Adventures don't always come easily to me because I like order, but I'm part of a family that's full of adventurers. And now I live in a place that beckons me to come out—out of my house and out of my comfort zone. My kids are growing up here, where the stars are easier to see and the trees shelter so much life. Since we've moved to the country, they've outgrown many pairs of shoes and pants, lost their teeth and Nerf bullets, and moved up so many notches on the growth charts.

I've grown up too. Greg and I have had some of the best years of our marriage here in the country, where my soul feels more relaxed and the pressure to keep too-quick a pace is less. I've bought muck boots, know the best entrances to the creek, and keep an eye on the turkey and deer who like to call our yard home too.

Spring on our property and in my soul makes it seem like life is always changing and being made new. But my faith remains in a constant God who faithfully ushers me into a connection with Him and my people in all the seasons. Hospitality allows us to adventure because we're anchored to where we've been, where we are, and the unknown that's still to come. Through it all, God is unchanging and asks us to seek Him all of our days.

STORY OF SHARED LIFE
AMANDA CONQUERS

Four years ago, I loaded up my baby, two extra car seats, and headed to a mosque to pick up an Afghani refugee and her two daughters. I remember driving over there, stomach in knots, wondering how I had gotten myself into this.

I knew nothing about Middle Eastern culture. I'd never heard of her first language (Pashto), much less known one word of it. I wasn't even sure I could pronounce her name right.

It all started when I saw the picture in my newsfeed of a child washed up on the Mediterranean shore. It made me weep. I read up on the Syrian refugee crisis—millions displaced while I was unaware. I began to pray over this one issue daily. Then I discovered a local Christian organization working with refugees just two cities from me. Still moved by the enormity of the crisis, I called and asked how I could help. One day they called back and said there was a refugee—an Afghani woman and her two young kids—abandoned by an abusive husband. Could I help? Would I host them? Would I collect furniture and essentials for them? I said yes.

If you want to know the truth, I didn't say yes because I am some kind of super Christian who oozes good deeds. I definitely didn't say yes because I am good at organizing charity events. I said yes because, well, I was already invested by my prayers and I was curious what God could do with me and my family. Truly, curiosity might be the closest virtue we sinners-saved-by-grace can get to courage. Someone once worked this into a beatitude of sorts: "Blessed are the curious, for they shall have adventures."

Indeed.

The best adventures are the ones we live when we are curious enough to follow the Lord wherever He leads.

I spent the day with Mariam and her two little girls. When I tried to make lunch, fabulous host that I am, I stood in the fridge staring at my only lunch meat choice—ham—suddenly remembering that Muslims don't eat pork. But she saw my eggs and wanted to make us lunch instead. Maybe this makes me a terrible host, but I let her. We watched our kids play, and we smiled knowingly at each other. While my kids taught hers the delicate art of blanket-fort building, Mariam shared her broken story in broken English. I cried with her and prayed over her.

When they left, I grabbed Mariam by the hand and called her friend. She looked me in the eyes and called me sister.

I got to help that precious family get settled in their new life. Our church rallied and furnished her whole apartment—from couch to kitchen utensils to toys for the girls. My kids still remember the visits to Mariam's apartment during that first year, snacking on raw nuts and dried fruits and sipping on delicious loose-leaf Afghan tea. I think she taught me more about hospitality than I ever did her. I felt like I was fumbling and unsure, but all hospitality required was that I say yes and follow the love of Christ. I'm so glad I did.

Amanda Conquers *is a cop's wife, mom to four, and an anxiety-struggler learning to be an overcomer. She writes at amandaconquers.com.*

Hospitality Celebrates

Birthdays can be hospitality at its finest.

We usually spread out celebrations around here, especially in May when end-of-the-school festivities are crowding our calendar. In that same month, Cate and I both have birthdays, there's Mother's Day to celebrate, and soccer for Ben and Rachel is usually still happening.

My 36th birthday was one of my favorites, especially the night I celebrated two days after my actual birthday with my friends. Earlier on the day we met for dinner at a local Mexican restaurant, I unexpectedly met Rachel's birth mom on the phone. I didn't even know that's what was happening when I answered the phone from a friend who connected me to her. I answered her questions about what a local, private adoption could look like for her and she invited me to an ultrasound the following week. That day I also received other news about a lake house we were selling and another one we were in the process of buying as a vacation rental, Ben was recovering from a tonsillectomy, and I was in the midst of planning an upcoming mission trip to Guatemala.

In all my personal excitement, I didn't even realize I had picked the local Mexican restaurant to gather with my friends on Cinco de Mayo. The crowd matched my internal adrenaline and we ended up lingering at the table once we got one because time with those friends was as satisfying as the queso.

I grocery shopped on my 37th birthday. It was a Tuesday in the middle of a busy season for our family. Cate was finishing third grade and Ben had made it to the end of kindergarten. We'd all survived and maybe even thrived as we added a new person to our family about a month after Ben started kindergarten. We had a new groove as a family of five. The week ahead held birthday party preparations for my girl turning nine, end-of-the-school extras like class parties and Teacher Appreciation Week, and some of my own celebrating, of course.

I had a really long list: ingredients to make chicken enchiladas for the teachers for Teacher Appreciation Week and then double for my own family, gifts cards for presents, diapers in a bigger size because Rachel was growing before my eyes, baby formula, toppings for the pancake bar Cate wanted for her Pippi Longstocking-themed birthday party, and, well, food for meals and snacks.

Food might be my love language. I used to think it was gift giving. And then quality time started to matter more. I still really love and feel loved knowing someone thought of me, took the time to get me something, and made plans with me.

But food.

Greg brought me a cinnamon roll from a local bakery that morning for my 37th birthday. My best friend planned dinner with some of my other friends later in the week so we could celebrate together. Even when it's not my birthday, I like to lunch with my friends. I plan gatherings with adoptive moms around a table at a local restaurant that also has a ball pit. Among favorite blessings as a new mom were when friends showed up with meals, so that's what I do for other new moms.

I'm telling you, food may be my love language. And birthdays.

Of course, there's something sacred about sharing meals and our real lives around a table. So sacred that after God made covenants with people, they ate. Jesus calls Himself the bread of life (John 6:35) and multiplies fishes (Matthew 14:13-21) so people know what it's like to feel full beyond their stomachs. We eat at weddings and birthday parties. We bring food after funerals and births.

Most importantly, we celebrate Jesus' sacrifice on the cross with Holy Communion. Our church does this weekly, but I know frequency varies from church to church. Christ followers know this simple, traditional meal is life changing. We remember Jesus gathering with His disciples for one last supper. We remember Jesus knowing His time on earth was ending and displaying faithfulness to His Father's plan. We remember His acts of dying and rising again and how that changes our futures forever. Communion is truth fulfilled.

My life is full in the best kind of ways. My 30s may have been my favorite decade. Perhaps that's why I wasn't bothered to grocery shop on my 37th birthday. I also knew there were meals coming later that week that I didn't have to make. Happy birthday to me.

To celebrate my 40th birthday, I knew I wanted to gather some old friends. Four dear friends (and three of their husbands and kids) joined my family at our lake house to do just that. They brought gifts, memories, and all the food we needed to feed our party of 23 people. Jaclyn, Sarah, Katie, and Bekah hadn't all met before, but I have histories with them that span decades, literally. Some of our stories have overlapped, but I knew this was the right group of people to gather together.

Starting in 1990, Katie was my next-door-neighbor-turned-best-friend for all of middle and high school and we remain friends across the state who wish we were still neighbors. Bekah and I also were friends in middle and high school. We swam together, she introduced me to country music, and we continue to gather at Christmastime and other times we have extra time when we're visiting my mom in Louisville. (Fun side note: I encouraged her and her now-husband to date, so they blame me and thank me in the same breath. I've actually known her husband Barrett longer than anyone who was at my lake house that weekend!)

Jaclyn and I met in college and had intersecting friends starting in the fall of 1998. We actually got closer after college, got married the same summer, walked through infertility and all the early days of motherhood together, and now miss each other if we go too many days without hanging out. Our husbands and kids are tight too.

Sarah walked into our church in May 2009, pregnant with Davey who would become my Ben's first friend, and we've basically been friends since. She's since moved four hours away, but we have an ongoing, never-ending text conversation that brings me so much joy.

Jaclyn and Katie put together a book of blessings and memories from all kinds of people in my life. Jaclyn gave me other goodies and helped organize the whole weekend. Sarah gave me a felt letter board with a sweet message already displayed. Katie made me a T-shaped shelf that's already hanging on my wall. Bekah bought my dinner when us girls went out for Mexican food one of the nights together. And, no, it wasn't Cinco de Mayo this time.

Our boys fished and caught enough bluegill and catfish to feed us lunch on Sunday. The older girls made friendship bracelets, had a sleepover in the basement one night, and helped us keep track of the little girls. We went on some boat rides, laughed at memories, reminisced with old stories, and ate well.

My soul was so filled with these new memories with old friends.

The celebrating continued the following Monday when some of my friends I know from my kids' school gathered for breakfast together. It was such a sweet way to begin the new week celebrating some more. Forty certainly had me reflective and craving all the quality time with people I love. Perhaps quality time does trump food ever so slightly as my love language.

I wanted to celebrate with my people, but God knew I would need to be filled to the brim with love and support as the week continued. God saw beyond my 40th birthday.

My dad went into cardiac arrest four days after I turned forty, one day after Cate turned twelve, and five days before Mother's Day. He passed away about thirty-five hours later on a Thursday.

He had been without oxygen three different times—for an undetermined amount of time when he went into cardiac arrest, on the way to the hospital in the ambulance, and again in the emergency room. His body never recovered, and I watched him stop breathing while hooked to a ventilator and lots of medicines in an Indianapolis hospital.

My relationship with my dad was complicated. For years, I've grieved not having the kind of relationship I wish we had. I spent many years being resentful that I wasn't a priority and couldn't figure out why he didn't want to spend time with my family or well as my siblings and their families. Before he died, I tried to forgive him and share my life with him, even from a physical and emotional distance.

Regardless of the complications, he was my dad. Right after I was filled from my birthday, I found myself unexpectedly grieving. As Dad was unresponsive in the hospital bed, I learned things about his life in Indianapolis I didn't know. I found myself beneath a cloud of emotions.

With three kids, the end of the school year, and my everyday life, I wasn't able to be buried beneath the cloud, but then when I slowed down, the grief was close. Grief is tricky. And I'm so grateful I was filled to the brim with love and support before I had to begin to navigate my dad's death.

I have questions I wish I could ask him. I want to hold onto hope for a little longer. I remember him as an innovative educator who created an environment at an elementary school for most of my childhood and then at a nearby middle school that teachers, parents, and students loved. He excelled in his profession.

Three of the friends who gathered at my lake house knew my dad. We had actually talked about some childhood memories involving him just days before he died. God was preparing me. I didn't know it then, but I found comfort in his death being sandwiched between so much life.

STORY OF SHARED LIFE
AMANDA PENNINGTON

Small towns in America love celebrating big events in their history. Small businesses and ministries that thrive do, too.

For the last 50 years, surrounded by the campus of Murray State University, two houses have been the home to Murray Christian Fellowship. Students who wanted to study the Bible and fellowship together throughout the week started this ministry. What started in an upstairs apartment grew into a ministry able to purchase its own house. MCF had a sweet neighbor named Mrs. Whitnah, who later in her life gave her home to the ministry as well. Out of that second house grew an additional ministry supporting pregnant women and families, known as Life House Care Center. When MCF grew too big, the second house for a time served as a coffee shop to the local community, and currently provides affordable housing for university students involved at the ministry.

In 2018, I had the pleasure of planning and hosting a huge celebration of the first 50 years this ministry has served Murray State students. We filled both front yards with more than 120 people, carnival games that all ages enjoyed, and food catered by a local business. We honored all the people who have supported this ministry and celebrated the many friendships and families that began at this property. We told stories of how those individuals have spread across the world sharing the hospitality and love of Christ to everyone they meet. Every person who has walked through MCF's doors has been changed in big and small ways and now they are out sharing life, meals, friendships, Bible studies, late night conversations, and their own homes with others they meet.

We can't wait to see what a huge eternal impact this small-town ministry has made, although we get to see a piece of that legacy now.

In MCF's early years, when the students who formed the ministry had graduated and no longer fit into the college demographic, those same people bonded together again and formed a local church so they could continue worshipping together. Now, decades later, those same friends have ministered to many more generations of students as well as the local community through worship services on Sundays and Wednesdays, held Vacation Bible School in the summers, hosted guest speakers literally from around the world, and put on concerts with musicians such as Jason Gray to benefit an overseas mission trip.

This is the church I call home. Personally, I think even though Sunday is the biggest thing we do, our cell groups are the best thing we do. We currently have groups that each are made up of four to five families who meet in members' homes, share meals, worship together, have Bible studies, and serve the church and local community.

These groups are a perfect example of hospitality and they cultivate deep friendships and give us a taste of the family the Kingdom of God provides! These friendships have been an absolute blessing to us personally, and have at times been just as close as blood family, providing encouragement and support in every possible way. Meeting together every week is definitely a celebration of how good our God is!

__Amanda Pennington__ met her husband, Payton Pennington, at this ministry, and even though they enjoy traveling and visiting friends from MCF who have moved away, they know God has called them to keep Murray their home.

Summer

Hospitality is not to change people, but to offer them space where change can take place.

Henri Nouwen

Hospitality Nourishes

Baby Rachel woke me up about ninety minutes before my alarm went off for the last day of school for her big brother and sister. I had a million things to do, yet I kept trying to decide if I should go back to sleep. Instead I decided to sit in the rocker thinking about how God surprised us with this baby girl who is growing up before our very eyes. She fell back asleep quickly, but I didn't want to lay her back down quite yet.

I want to remember every detail. I want to treasure the moments, but sometimes I get overwhelmed by the day-to-day and miss the big picture. Sometimes I don't know how to respond to my big kids' imperfections when I know there's an important character-molding lesson to be had because I'm still dealing with my own imperfections. And then sometimes it all just makes sense. Sometimes it's good to be alert and have the time to sit, think, prepare for the others to rise . . . and hold this baby who is somehow already eight months old.

I ended up using the quiet to get some things done around the house. The dirty dishes were loaded and the washing machine was cycling again.

"Did I sleep long enough, Momma?" My six-year-old boy said as he peeped around the kitchen corner, wearing only shorts and wrapping himself in his beloved night-night blanket.

"Um, no not really, but the sleeping in needs to start tomorrow," I say, trying to be welcoming but a little disturbed he's awake early after we let him stay up later the night before.

This season seemed new. Bedtime is less rushed with big kids who wash their own hair and put on their own pajamas. Somehow I have kids finishing kindergarten and third grade along with this baby who epitomizes joy.

Greg heard that people were up and proposed a last-day-of-school breakfast out. So we got ready and had cinnamon rolls, muffins, and sausage sandwiches for breakfast. And then I grocery shopped before 8 a.m.

I know some of my summer days will involve grocery shopping with all three. And that's not even something I dread. But still I'm grateful on this last day of school that we won't have to go anywhere tomorrow.

I love summer. I love the foods we eat, the slower mornings, the afternoons by the pool, the white spaces on our calendar, and the sunshine. I'm teaching my kids to love these things too. On the afternoon my big kids finished fourth and first grades, we celebrated the beginning of the season we all love . . . with a trip to Kroger on the way home from school.

It's no joke the amount of food my kids want to eat when they're home. Breakfast. Snack. Lunch. Snack. Snack. Dinner. Snack. And we like to have friends over, and those friends like to eat snacks and meals too.

Armed with big kids still dressed in their school uniforms, a toddler who adores her much-older siblings, and a lengthy grocery list on my iPhone, we headed into Kroger. The thing about big kids is they're helpful. They can read and fetch items. They can talk to the toddler. They can hold the list and tell me what's next. They may not have loved spending the first hour of their summer break in Kroger, but I loved having them with me, reminding me of the days when they were little but making me thankful we've all grown up.

We stocked up on Gatorade, cereal, eggs, sandwich fixings, Ritz crackers, and fruit. Honestly, I didn't have any dinners planned, but there's always spaghetti to fall back on and the freezer full of meat. Plus, if I'm being honest, I'd rather be poolside than hovering over a hot stove during summer break.

Of course, my people have to eat—and they will. We left Kroger on that mid-May afternoon with a cart full as proof. The kids fell into their normal roles of being unloading helpers when we got home, carrying in bags as I started to put away the groceries.

And then it was time to celebrate school being out for the summer. With a snack, of course.

The first summer we had a pool I tried not to overdo the pool pictures on social media, but that's how we happily spent our summer. I like to document everyday life so I can remember. So, there were pool pictures.

On an Instagram post about another afternoon at the pool, my college friend Missy commented with some hospitality wisdom: "It seems like there's a different set of kids in every group of pool photos you post. I love it! I grew up with a pool in the backyard and having friends over every day to swim was just part of life. It's an excellent way to make hospitality a normal thing for your kids!" Her words summed up what God did on our porch and around our pool that summer. Hospitality being a normal part of life is something I hope continues for many summers to come.

Around here, the pool and porch were good excuses to invite people over to our house and into our lives. The kids who came over made memories while they swam together, but connections beyond the pool were made.

"Who's coming over today?" is a near-daily question from my kids. I want my house to be a gathering place for people and their stories, and that first summer with the pool taught me some things about that:

1. Feeding people can be simple. Get carry out. Order pizza. Have a taco bar. Buy the birthday cake. Host a potluck. Nobody cares that you didn't make the chicken salad from scratch.

2. Keep items on hand to make hospitality happen. We have a caddy of plastic ware right next to the stack of paper plates and an extra fridge stocked almost entirely with drinks. I keep Wyler's Italian Ice in the freezer to share with friends who come to spend the afternoon at the pool.

3. Connections happen when we let them. More than once that summer I wanted to break out with that children's song: "Make new friends, but keep the gold. One is silver and the other's gold." This was especially true when my long-time best friend told a newer friend she had prayed

for her when she was growing her family through adoption.

4. Kids are kids regardless of their backgrounds. Kids don't care about skin color, whether adoption or foster care is part of their family's story, or what kind of house they call home. They make up games and play them together.

5. Hospitality can happen anywhere. You can meet poolside (obviously!), at a restaurant, or a picnic table near a playground. Make the setting whatever works for you and whoever you're inviting.

Of course, hospitality doesn't have to involve a party. We like parties and gatherings around here. But hospitality can mean making a phone call or sending a text. It may mean showing up with a meal or a McDonald's Coke. It's about letting someone in your life and being willing to walk into theirs.

Hospitality nourishes, so let's take care of each other. It really doesn't have to be complicated, so let's jump in together.

STORY OF SHARED LIFE
ASHLEE YOUNG

Better is a neighbor who is near than a brother who is far
away.

Proverbs 27:10b

I have always loved meeting new people, but I never knew how
much I loved being around my family and how scary it was to
connect with others until we moved to another state for my husband
to attend graduate school. Being 311 miles away from family and
friends, I saw the importance and need of finding a community
around us. We quickly got involved with a local church and started
attending a weekly small group. Many meals and parties (we loved
celebrating together) were shared.

Fast forward four and a half years later when we had our
daughter Leela. She came so quickly that we didn't have time to call
anyone, not even our family. Everyone woke up to a big surprise the
next day and made arrangements to drive five hours north. In the
meantime, the first person to meet our little girl was my mentor,
Mindi, someone who had known me less than five years but who
had prayed for me, counseled me through hard times, and fed me so
many meals. (She makes the best cream cheese bars.) She also
created the Meal Train for our new little family that started when
we got home from the hospital.

Our parents both had responsibilities at home and were only
able to stay overnight with their new granddaughter, so we
depended on those who were near us. Though our parents took
good care of us when they were here, our local church and
colleagues fed us more than we could have ever imagined. Even
students I had taught and their parents brought us meals. I don't
remember cooking much in Leela's first few weeks, but I do

remember the conversations, the encouragement, and the love I felt from those who visited and brought meals.

I am forever thankful for the relationships we formed while my husband was in graduate school and pray to be that person when others need someone or a meal. Anytime I see a Meal Train on Facebook, I sign up. What could have been the hardest time in our lives, ended up being the best weeks of our lives. I give credit to food. Food brings people together. Food builds friendships. Food celebrates new lives.

Ashlee Young *is wife to Jeff, a stay-at-home mommy to Leela, and likes adventures, tea, and a good book.*

HOSPITALITY MINISTERS

Years before we had a third child and a pool, we had friends over three nights in a row one week in June. The agendas were different: Game of Things and Settlers of Catan with our best friends one night, discussion of Randy Alcorn's *In Light of Eternity* with our small group the next, and then USA's World Cup game with soccer-loving friends. Yes, we've all got extroverted tendencies in this house.

All the gatherings involved food. And they all involved real life.

Nothing was perfect but I wouldn't have changed a thing.

Crumbs were left on the floor and counters had residue from various dishes. People shared their struggles and asked for advice and prayer around our table. Kids tracked in water that dropped from their clothes after an impromptu water fight.

I feel blessed in the walls of my house—even among the messes.

Sometimes sadness and conflict and heartache seem overwhelming outside my house and I want to cling to this life we've built here. Sure, sometimes I'm loud and rock the peace, but I love what God does here, when it's our little family and when we invite others in. Those with whom we share life bring their own messes inside when they track in dirt and share their hard days. And that's exactly how it's supposed to be. I don't want to do this life alone and I don't want the people around me to either. God's word even encourages a hospitable lifestyle: "Above all, keep loving one another earnestly, since love covers a multitude of sins. Show hospitality to one another without grumbling" (1 Peter 4:8-9).

Sometimes hospitality involves sacrifice. The way you open your home and your life in the summer probably isn't the same as in the fall days. Weather and schedules factor into that for sure. Maybe you have to give up something you want to do so you can show up where you need to be. Maybe you need to stop streaming a Netflix show so you can host small group or dinner with your neighbors. Maybe bedtime will get postponed, you'll spend more than you budgeted, or you have to have a hard conversation.

As a host, I prepare to have visitors. That could mean cleaning, cooking, or planning an activity. Preparations may also be mental and emotional because vulnerability does require effort. Our preparations here on earth are nothing compared to what Jesus has done and is doing for us. In John 14:2-3, we get a glimpse of the place Jesus is preparing for us. There are many rooms, also known as abiding places. I love what David Guzik wrote about these verses in his commentary: "Love prepares a welcome. With love, expectant parents prepare a room for the baby. With love, the hostess prepares for her guests. Jesus prepares a place for His people because He loves them and is confident of their arrival."[6] Jesus is ready for us. I want to be ready to let others in—both through the door and into my life.

Even with preparations required, our relationships will always be better for opening up our homes and lives. People are changed through connection. Sometimes relationships change like the seasons; other times people become so intertwined our lives are never ever the same. But we sure do need each other.

When I read *The Ministry of Ordinary Places*, I felt like Shannan Martin peeked into my life. Her words made her part cheerleader and part wise older sister in my life. I could quote countless passages for you, but this one especially speaks to why hospitality matters: "Hospitality, the urge to gather, is hardwired into our spiritual and relational DNA. It might look a little different from person to person, but in this one way, we recognize our shared lineage of potlucks and patios, long nights where the wick burns down to an ember and the kids invite some small catastrophe. Despite all the mess and unpredictability, I'm positive it is worth taking some risks and making some mistakes to cultivate a consistent rhythm of welcome and belonging in our homes."[7]

Sure, hospitality is a risk. During the annual flu season or the surprising coronavirus epidemic that shut down so much in the spring of 2020, inviting others in may have brought some germs. Emotional risks, such as misunderstanding someone's point of view or being vulnerable with someone new, also are part of sharing life with real people. But with risk comes reward. Maybe you accidentally shared germs, but I bet you also found common ground. Perhaps sharing a hard story for the first time was scary, but next time the same story will come a little easier. And sometimes the risks are the rewards.

I love how Joanna Gaines' *Magnolia Journal* regularly encourages people to share their tables and their lives and acknowledges that risks may surprise us: "The definition of a risk is a situation that exposes you to danger. But danger doesn't always look like we might expect: You could be in danger of falling in love. You could be in danger of having the best day of your life. You could be in danger of getting everything you want. You could be in danger of laughing so hard it hurts. You could be in danger of finding a person who knows what you're thinking before you say a word. You could be in danger of loving a song so much you have to sing it out loud, as loud as you can. You could be in danger of opening your heart instead of closing it."[8]

Of course, none of us are perfect in fostering friendship, but even so we are better together. We're given lots of chances to do the right thing, start the next necessary conversation, or add another chair around a table. Don't let fears of messes—in your home or your heart—stop you from facing the risks and discovering the rewards.

Randy Alcorn writes in *In Light of Eternity*: "Heaven will cleanse us of sin and error, but it won't erase our lives and memories. The people we've known here, who God has sent to impact our lives, are His gift to us, as we are His gift to them. To forget these people would be to forget God's grace and provision."[9]

One day we'll be cleaned up and washed off eternally. Our messes are temporary, but right now matters forever. Our people and their hearts matter.

Of course, sometimes right now means remembering priorities and not inviting people over. I've caught myself apologizing to people: I'm sorry I haven't been on the computer much, but here's that thing I told you I would send. I'm sorry I missed your call, but I was doing this with my kids. I'm sorry for the delay, but we had a busy weekend together. I need to stop that. As soon as the words are out of my mouth, I hear it: I'm telling them I'm sorry because I was doing my first and most important calling. That shouldn't require an apology. Obviously, I'm also a believer in doing what I say I will do and helping people, but even those good things have been known to interrupt my priorities.

My husband, my kids, and even myself are part of God's kingdom. To serve them—and, yes, even myself sometimes—well means I am serving God and His people. Ministry begins at home and should thrive at home. In a hard season of remembering where God has me, I read *Present Over Perfect* by Shauna Niequist, who spoke truth into my life: "You don't have to sacrifice your spirit, your joy, your soul, your family, your marriage on the altar of ministry. Just because you have the capacity to do something doesn't mean you have to do it. Management, organization, speaking and traveling: you must ask not only what fruit they bring to the world, but what fruit they yield on the inside of your life and your heart."[10]

Obviously, I certainly don't think our service and love should stop at the walls of our house, but I do believe it begins here and then overflows beyond. So many voices are screaming—often times not intentionally—just the opposite. There are always opportunities to do and give and go, but not all those opportunities are meant for me.

I want my days to reflect my priorities: God, husband, kids, other people, in that order. That's a preparation I take seriously.

Some days I worry more about what chores my kids have finished and what their behavior has said about them than the condition of their hearts. Some days I judge my worth based on my productivity and give myself points for the number of errands and chores I can successfully complete. Too often my husband gets what energy is left over once the sun has set, the dirty dishes have been cleaned, and the kids were rushed off to bed. Other days I serve my husband well and am kind to my kids. Some days I truly connect with people and don't worry about my to-do list. Other days I see the mountains of laundry and the kitchen messes as opportunities to serve. When my priorities are in order—on my calendar but especially in my heart—then I'm always amazed that God seems to provide what I need to be a responsible adult. That's when the people in my home—both the ones who live here and the ones who visit—are more at peace, even if there are still crumbs on the floor.

Love covers many messes as hospitality ministers.

STORY OF SHARED LIFE
KATIE CUNNINGHAM

The internet and social media have allowed us to see every tragedy on both large and small scales. We see natural disasters, but we also know about every case of cancer, stillborn baby, untimely death, suicide, and the list goes on. It can be so overwhelming. I don't believe we were meant to bear the burdens of the whole world but rather the burdens of our own communities.

Depending on our personalities we can respond in different ways to all this information and heartache. If you are someone who struggles with anxiety and or depression, all of this tragedy can overwhelm you. It also can hinder you from enjoying the blessings that God has given you for fear that those blessings can be taken away. On the other end of the spectrum, you may be someone who can handle all the information coming at you but the sheer volume of it can cause you to become numb. In this case we lose the ability to empathize with those nearest to us.

So what do we do? How do we combat this and still have an influential presence online but also meet the needs of our own community? I think we have to discipline ourselves to do this. Practical things we can do include:

1. Limit your time on social media outlets. Set time limits on your phone where you only check for thirty minutes to one hour each day.
2. Have one day a week where you do not look at social media.
3. If you do see something on social media affecting someone in your actual community, pick up the phone and call them or visit. A phone call or a visit ministers more to a person than a comment on a post ever could.
4. Limit your time reading and watching the news.

As I am writing this I am living in the middle of the coronavirus pandemic. Community only exists online and the best way to love your neighbor is to stay away from them. I have praised God for technology during this time, but I have also seen how it can never replace in-person community. I look forward to the day when I can turn off the screen to fully connect with all the people in my life. I anticipate the day when I can take a home-cooked meal, hold a new baby, visit a friend in the hospital, go to church, celebrate birthdays, gather around a table, go to a concert, chat in the grocery store, hug, laugh, mourn and dance side by side with those around me.

The early church provides us with the best example of meeting the needs of our community in Acts 2:42-47: "And they devoted themselves to the apostles' teaching and the fellowship, to the breaking of bread and the prayers. And awe came upon every soul, and many wonders and signs were being done through the apostles. And all who believed were together and had all things in common. And they were selling their possessions and belongings and distributing the proceeds to all, as any had need. And day by day attending the temple together and breaking bread in their homes, they received their food with glad and generous hearts, praising God and having favor with all the people. And the Lord added to their number day by day those who were being saved."

Katie Cunningham *is a pastor's wife who works in her home raising three sons and a daughter.*

Hospitality Interrupts

I don't love for my plans to be interrupted, but more than once those changes have been exactly what I needed. Yes, that's hard to admit, but God's been proving His timing to be superior to mine over and over again.

On my 37th birthday, my dear friend Sarah, who had moved four hours away a few months before, texted me to ask if I could swing by Culver's to pick up an ice cream cake she ordered for me. She knew I was meeting local friends for dinner and said she wanted to contribute a cake to the occasion. That's the kind of interruption I like in my day!

So I re-routed to Culver's. When I walked in the restaurant, Sarah was there waiting for me! She had her four kids in tow and they all were enjoying some ice cream. I cried right there in Culver's. We hung out for a while that afternoon—again an interruption that warmed my soul—and then Sarah joined us for dinner that night.

There wasn't actually a cake, but I'll take my friends gathered around a table to eat a dinner I didn't have to prepare as the best gift anyway. This was the year after we'd accidentally celebrated on Cinco de Mayo in a Mexican restaurant so we chose the local Thai restaurant instead. We laughed and talked and filled our souls while we filled our stomachs. I left that table full and grateful for friendships that sustain change and serve as foundations for so many of my memories.

Another interruption happened a couple months later for Sarah's birthday. Jaclyn and I planned to meet her in the middle, but then one of Sarah's kids woke up vomiting, so we rescheduled. The day it actually happened, Jaclyn and I drove 360 miles round trip with our kids to meet Sarah for lunch about halfway between the four hours that separate us. Sarah's van ended up breaking down, so Jaclyn and I kept all ten of the kids at a park while Sarah dealt with her van at a nearby auto repair shop. The park had a splash pad, which was ideal because it was 90-something degrees in the middle of July. Of course, we didn't have any swimsuits with us, but the kids played anyway. We gave them whatever drinks we had and ended up getting Icees on our way home several hours later.

The adventurous day unfolded in ways we obviously didn't anticipate, but it was one that bonded the best kind of friends—the ones who pile into minivans and drive toward each other and land in a location kind of in the middle, the ones who take care of each other, and the ones who are just crazy enough to do something like it again one day.

As moms, we have plenty of opportunities to use interruptions to care for and serve others, especially our little ones who have lots to say when we're in the middle of something else. All of us can make excuses and not choose what seems inconvenient. I have to remind myself sometimes, but those interruptions certainly can be blessings if we are able to set aside our expectations of what a situation should be.

In John 4:1-43, Jesus taught me something about seeing interruptions as ministry opportunities. He was passing through Samaria on His way from Judea to Galilee. "Wearied as he was from his journey" (verse 6), Jesus sat down at a well and a Samaritan woman came to draw water and Jesus asked her to give him a drink. They proceeded to have conversation about living water that eternally satisfies (verses 11-14). Jesus knew about her sinful past with five husbands and encouraged her to believe in the Messiah (verses 16-26).

Jesus' disciples asked questions about why He was talking to the woman because doing that interrupted culture norms, as well as what He was on course to do and what was expected of the Messiah. Yet because Jesus took the time to talk to her, "many Samaritans from that town believed in him because of the woman's testimony ..." (verse 39). More Samaritans came to Jesus and asked Him to stay with them and He did for two days (verse 40). And more people believed (verse 41).

People's lives were changed because Jesus saw an interruption as a ministry opportunity.

One of the biggest interruptions to my normal life came with spring in 2020. In an effort to avoid COVID-19 and do our part to protect others, we were healthy at home for twelve weeks before we started widening our social circle. But that meant we didn't socialize face-to-face with anyone beyond our family of five until the coronavirus risk dissipated. Other than the grocery store, I didn't go anywhere. Schools, restaurants, churches, non-essential businesses, and parks were closed. Talk about an interruption.

But I got to see God answer a prayer in my family. For years, I'd be praying for my kids to deepen their friendships with one another. They were four, ten, and turning thirteen at the time, and God gave me a miracle. Cate and Ben played basketball together by choice, even though their competitive spirits got the best of them at times. Cate taught Rachel to play some board games and allowed her younger sister in her usually-off-limits bedroom. Ben and Rachel were morning time buddies. All three made up games to play together on the trampoline. We played board games, explored creeks, watched movies together, and completed some home improvement projects. Hospitality happened in our home because our normal life was interrupted.

We gradually widened our circle, starting with my mother-in-law. Then we gathered with my mom, my siblings, and their families. Our best friends came over. My Bible study met on our porch. Our small group from church met in someone's backyard. The rhythm was different than before COVID slowed our lives and shut down much of our routine, but hospitality remained. I quickly remembered why we gather as a family, with extended relatives, and with friends who in so many ways are like family.

As I extended more invitations, I recognized how isolation is a real risk and exposing each other to community is important. What community looks like may change with circumstances that interrupted the usual flow, but being known is necessary. Once again, the *Magnolia Journal* spoke to hospitality: "The true reward of gathering is found in the risk of being real—and what's real within us, and between us, is not always so pretty. When we dare to expose the messy, uncurated parts of ourselves to others, it gives them the space to be more vulnerable. To be known deeply—like family—feels really, really good. Sometimes family can be untidy and untamed, but that feeling of belonging is hard to beat."[11]

Before we scoff at the interruptions in our days, let's remember those unexpected moments could bring a deeper sense of belonging.

STORY OF SHARED LIFE
SHELLY DIVINO

When I said yes to Jesus, I never imagined landing in a third-world country surrounded by a community to which I struggled to relate, let alone one with whom I was unable to communicate. I felt pretty confident I could create community anywhere, but then my husband and I found ourselves in the trials of life having to relearn the basics of living in a new culture. I went from throwing clothes in the washing machine to spending hours hand washing our clothes. Even the most basic daily tasks exhausted me beyond words, leaving the introvert in me running from every human interaction. Creating community was the last thing on my mind, yet it was everything for which my heart and soul longed.

God sees and He knows. When everything inside of me wanted to run away from people in hopes silence would restore my soul, He would so gracefully put us in a situation where we needed what someone else had. I needed to learn how to do the most basic tasks without the luxuries of America, so God brought people to show me how. In a place of need, those divine appointments became family. I remember one day being half-way through dinner when the gas tank ran out. Minutes later the local pastor showed up at our door simply to drop off a pizza. He didn't know our need. He didn't know my disappointment or frustration from the day. But he knew love. He knew our struggles being in a far-away land with no family to call. He showed up in our time of need. And just like that God built our community.

The community God built for us was not one I thought we needed. If I would have said no to the relationships God brought to me, I never would have been able to survive the new land. It took a new community to teach us to live. It took someone to translate. It took someone to teach. It took someone to watch our backs when we didn't know we were in need of protection.

During the COVID-19 outbreak I was racing back from the

United States to my family in Guatemala before the borders were to be shut indefinitely. I changed my flight to make it back in time, but the overwhelming fear of being stuck away from my family left me sleepless and anxious. Then at 3 o'clock in the morning I received a text from my friend who works in the Guatemala airport. She knew what was going on and kept me in the loop my whole journey. She told me what to expect and calmed my nerves. Even after she got off work, she waited outside in the parking garage to make sure I landed and was allowed into the country without being quarantined. She saw my need and she showed up.

Community is something we often take for granted. It's in the trials of life where we don't have the time or energy to create a community that God comes in and builds it for us. Sometimes life puts us in unwanted seasons. Sometimes trials come that we don't understand. Yet it is in the middle of those wilderness seasons where we find we have all we need. It's where we find the people around us need us as much as we need them. It's in our need where God builds our community.

Shelly Divido *is wife to Harry, mother to Hannah, missionary and founder of Light of the World Ministries, but, most importantly, a daughter to the King of Kings.*

HOSPITALITY BEFRIENDS

As I was reaching for the vegetable oil to put in my grocery cart, a stranger said, "Are you familiar with GMOs?"

Her tone was one of inquiry, so I politely said, "Not really," thinking she wanted advice.

Turns out she wanted to advise me: "GMOs are the greatest health concern facing our nation. Do you get on the computer? You should look it up. Canola oil is ..."

"Well, I'm getting vegetable oil." And I continued on down the baking aisle, thankful to have a pantry staple I'd been missing. Now I could make more brownies.

I had recently tried to substitute eggs in a boxed brownie mix with yogurt. I figured if I found the substitution on a baking website I was in the clear. Um, not so. The brownies were gooey and just not right. Google should have advised me better when I typed "substitute eggs in brownie mix." Something more blunt: Just don't do it. Wait until you have eggs.

My Facebook friends offered all kinds of guidance by recommending substitutions like black beans and flax seed as well as a brownie recipe involving chickpeas. People, if I don't have eggs, the likelihood of me having flax seed is nil. And while I like black beans, they belong in soups and fajitas. But I really do love Facebook and the broad community it provides when I need to know things.

A week or so later, I decided substituting the vegetable oil in another attempt at boxed brownies was too risky. There's a reason I make brownies from a box. And only the Ghiradelli kind. They're typically the dessert I take to new moms or friends who can benefit from a meal they didn't have to prepare.

Back to the stranger who wanted to talk about GMOs. In addition to being way too far up in my business, she actually asked me if I got on the computer as I was consulting my grocery list on my iPhone. Really, lady?

People have all kinds of opinions about pretty much anything—baking and eating habits, whether to use essential oils, what kind of milk to drink, why organic is best, whether sugar should be banned. It's fine to have opinions and create habits for your family. It's even fine to share your thoughts when the other person seems receptive to hearing them.

But boldness can come across as rudeness when absolutely no relationship has been established. This woman didn't even say hi before she launched into her lecture on GMOs, of which I retained zilch.

This applies to more than the bossy stranger in the grocery store. People spew hateful words on Facebook, falsely assuming their rants will change someone's political stance. Moms judge each other for parenting differently. The temptation to control seeps into marriages and friendships.

We'd all be better off if we looked for ways to encourage and love each other well rather than run over each other with our words. Most moms know biting words aren't much different than being struck in your ankles with the grocery cart your kid is driving recklessly behind you, so let's stop passing so much judgement and find more ways to be a good friend in everyday life.

1. Make plans. Invite someone over. Suggest a meeting at the park or coffee shop. Host other families and people in different seasons of life for dinner.

2. Text and call. Follow up if you know someone had an appointment or started a new job. Just ask how she is—and really listen.

3. Deliver dinner. This is a favorite of mine since I was blessed this way following the births of each of my kids. I like to take a casserole or soup earlier in the day so my friend can just bake/reheat it when she's ready to eat. Often I double it for my family too. Win-win.

4. Send real mail. I do this sometimes because, like the food delivery, I like it myself.

5. Include friends in your regular routine. Lunch together

after church. Find a shared interest, like sports or a board game. Befriend your kids' friends' parents.

6. Tell a friend if you miss her. Just because someone lives close doesn't mean we have to be all right with not actually seeing her.

7. Do it—just because. It could be anything. Bake them a dessert. Treat her to lunch. Send her flowers. Yes, celebrate birthdays or important dates, but also just celebrate her.

8. Offer to keep her kids. Maybe you know she's busy. Maybe you know she'd like a break. Maybe your kids want playmates. "Just because" works here too.

9. Share real life. Trust them with the hard things. Let them in when your house is a mess and your heart isn't much tidier. Reveal fears and dreams.

10. Make yourself available. This may mean asking if she needs anything from the grocery or carpooling. It could also mean incorporating any of the other nine things listed above, even if it interrupts what you had planned.

And perhaps don't share your passion for GMOs during your first meeting because true hospitality seeks to befriend others.

STORY OF SHARED LIFE
SHELLEY SAPP

Change has never been something I handle like a champ. I prefer to have my calendar laid out clearly every day and expect it to go smoothly—no bumps, no detours. Disruptions to my schedule aren't welcome and when they do come, I don't typically handle it well. Major changes and small ones alike make my stomach clench and my mind reel. Finding out we were expecting our first baby caused tears of panic. It was a change and a huge unknown. Moving across town and making all four of my kids switch schools caused me sleepless nights. Only me, mind you, the rest of the family was fine! I even pitched a toddler-esque fit at Costco one day when I realized they'd stopped carrying my favorite brand of sausage. What would I do without my sausage?!

So imagine my angst when we realized God was calling us to move halfway across the country. We'd spent all sixteen years of our marriage building community with our church friends, neighbors, and co-workers. One of my spiritual gifts is hospitality so our home was consistently buzzing with activity. I thrived on planning and hosting big gatherings and hearing the conversations and laughter that accompany them.

Now we had to start from scratch. We knew no one in our new town (or the state for that matter) and I certainly didn't want it to take years to build a network of friends like it took back home. So I stepped outside of my comfort zone and made the first move. I posted on a local Facebook group and immediately connected with someone from the same Indiana town from which we'd just moved! We met at a park, had a great time, and she invited me to join her Bunco group. I'd never played Bunco a day in my life and going to a social gathering with a group of strangers was not my idea of a great Saturday night! But I showed up, and when I walked in and someone immediately shouted my name. A completely different lady I'd met the day before at high school registration was there and remembered me! My heart leapt and I immediately felt a sense of belonging. She introduced me to everyone like we were old friends and made me feel at ease.

We chatted, ate lots of food, and got to know each other. I had a great time and didn't hesitate when the next Bunco date rolled around. I even volunteered to host this group of strangers that were fast becoming friends. Yes, it would have been easier to stay at home that first night. Yes, I could have easily let my insecurities win and keep me away. But I didn't just want to meet new people. I *needed* to meet new people—to start developing a new sense of community and one I feel like we belong to.

I'm so thankful for that group of "strangers." My best friend here came from that group. Those ladies gave me the confidence I needed to start over, to create new relationships, to belong. And even though the move itself caused plenty of change, anxiety, and tears, it was without a doubt the right move for our family and I wouldn't change it for the world.

Shelley Sapp is a stay-at-home mother of four currently living near Colorado Springs, Colorado.

HOSPITALITY SHARES

Jenn and I became friends one summer because we kept running into each other in our small town. Our oldest girls were invited to the same birthday party. We both picked up vegetables from a local farm each week. We talked when we'd see each other and then started to plan to see each other. This was all before any of our kids were in elementary school. Jenn and her family have since moved away from the small town that brought us together, I've added another kid to the mix, and most of our kids are in elementary and middle schools now.

To Jenn's middle daughter, I was the mom who could supply a snack at any moment wherever we were. While this wasn't necessarily true, she has these big, brown, beautiful eyes that make me always want to produce fruit snacks or crackers from my pocket. In reality, there were numerous times I happened to have a snack stored in my stroller while Jenn and I walked laps around the park, usually with at least our two youngest in tow. In our collection of five children (at the time) between us, Adeline was in the middle. She's in the middle of three girls in her own family and she was in the middle of our combined families too. My boy, the only boy in our group, is a year younger than Adeline. But, goodness, he adored her.

Meanwhile I won her over with my snacks. I believe with my whole heart that Jenn fed her children, but somehow Adeline was often hungry when I was around. She would tell me she was hungry, so I looked at her mom and asked with my eyes, "Is it okay to give her this granola bar?"

One of my favorite times was when we were playing at the park when Chloe was five, Cate was almost five, Adeline was three, Ben was two, and Piper was just months old. Multiple kids complained of thirst. Sure, it was hot, but the girl-heavy population was overly dramatic. Once they chilled out, I remembered I had some bottles

of Grape Propel that never made it from my trunk to my refrigerator after a recent grocery trip. I carried a few from my trunk to the
playground and you'd have thought I was lavishing treasures upon
them. Their thirst was quenched and Adeline's faith that I can
supply food and drink to meet her desires remained. And, really,
how better to be a friend to a preschool girl?

This same summer I celebrated my 33rd birthday, and I'm
pretty sure Adeline helped her mom pick out my present. Crafty
Jenn had her girls pick out fabric so they could make me a reusable
shopping bag. She also unnecessarily restocked my supply of snacks
with some new-to-me treats. Along with this totally thoughtful and
practical gift was a note: "Thank you for feeding my spirit and
Adeline's tummy!" She gave me credit for feeding her child, literally,
and her spirit, but truth is being with Jenn always fed my soul too.
That's the beauty of real-life hospitality—everyone leaves the park,
or wherever else you are, full in every way.

One afternoon a few months after I quenched Adeline's thirst at
the park, we tie-dyed T-shirts on Jenn's concrete patio, which sounds
like a really brave activity now that I'm thinking back! As we were
leaving their house, Cate stuffed her dress pockets with pistachios
and grapes that had been sitting out as a community snack. And
then Chloe handed her and Ben packages of string cheese. You
would have thought Cate was unsure she'd have enough food for her
next meal. All I could do was look at Jenn, admit I had no idea what
my daughter was thinking, and thank her for sharing.

Jenn shared her snacks and her tie-dye kit that day. Other days I
shared my snacks. We've walked laps at the park. We've eaten meals
at each other's houses. We've met at restaurants. We've talked about
our dreams. We've problem solved even when we weren't sure of the
solution.

Through it all, Jenn and I forged a friendship that nourished my
soul. Friendship truly is the best kind of sharing there is, especially
when it happens around a table, even a picnic table.

Hospitality shares what we have. Maybe that's a meal or a visit.
Perhaps that's a disposable pan of Ghiradelli brownies. Even Jesus
shared his presence with his friends in John 12:1-8. Jesus knew His

earthly death was coming, yet He went to visit his friends Mary, Martha, and Lazarus with whom He shared a history. You may remember He raised Lazarus from the dead; talk about a bonding experience! Now, his friends were hosting Him. Martha served. Lazarus reclined with Him at the table. Mary used her expensive oil on His feet. They appreciated Him and shared what they had. Together they got to feast, fellowship, and forge deeper friendships.

When we weren't at parks, Jenn and I liked to meet at breakfast tables. We started a tradition of taking each other out for breakfast near our birthdays—which, really, is like the adult version of food sharing. One February morning, I had invited her to a local restaurant where the booths are worn and the walls have absorbed so many small-town secrets. She got an omelet and some toast, and I got an omelet with different ingredients and biscuits. After enjoying food and conversations, I went to pay and remembered once I got to the cashier that I didn't have any cash to pay our bill at this restaurant that didn't take credit cards. I had to ask Jenn to pay for our breakfast—the one I invited her to for her birthday. She dug cash out of her purse with no hesitation. And we sometimes still laugh about it.

Jenn moved not too long after that, and now our shared meals are mostly memories, although we did get to meet at the same local restaurant that now accepts cards during one recent Christmas break. We found our places on a worn booth bench and talked like we had been at the park with our kids just the week before. That pick-up-where-you-left-off feeling marks a fulfilling friendship where real life has been shared.

STORY OF SHARED LIFE
MARY JOST

I am an introvert who gets anxious about the thought of hosting groups of people at my house. I don't throw my kids birthday parties because I always worry about different groups of people from my life feeling the awkwardness of intermingling together with people they don't necessarily know. I don't do well with socially awkward situations and I just assume others don't as well. I tend to over assume that just because I would be uncomfortable others will be as well. I also get mentally worn out thinking of trying to talk to every single person and make them feel like they are not being left out. If anyone comes to my house, I try to always make them feel at ease and welcome.

I am blessed with a huge yard and a very small house. Other members in my family have much bigger houses and spaces to gather indoors than I do. Yet, somehow, my husband and I are the ones who always host family parties, get-togethers, and holiday gatherings. Throughout the years we have been able to see the huge blessing it does to our hearts to host my large family. While we definitely do not have the largest house, we have the most child-proofed house. When family gathers at our house I am not stressed out that my children are not touching things they are not supposed to be touching or playing with things or in areas that are not meant for them to play with. At our house, they have free rein to play because they cannot destroy anything. The backyard is a great place for them to run around and be kids. They don't have to worry about being quiet outdoors.

Now more than a decade into marriage, I have slowly started inviting friends over to hang out during school breaks and in the summertime. I have started realizing it does not matter what size my house is. Instead, the intention is what matters. I try to be intentional with my friendships and I want the same for my kids' friendships. I want people to feel comfortable when they come over to my house. I want them to sit back on the recliner or couch while we chat while our kids have fun making messes that will eventually be cleaned up. I always have snacks on hand for little friends who come to our house. I want them to feel like my house is a place they and their parents can come to and relax while having fun.

Hospitality is about more than letting people inside and physically hosting them. Hospitality is sharing your heart with others because you care. Hospitality is intentional.

Mary Jost is a Jesus-loving Georgian who loves hiking with her family, traveling to Disney World, and going to concerts.

Hospitality Lingers

One summer I learned to linger longer.

Yes, some of this lesson was learned poolside, where I've relaxed with friends or a novel while dirty dishes and laundry piles waited. But that's not the only place I've lingered.

Almost-nightly games of rummy with my ten-year-old girl who stays up later than the other two kids helped me linger in that season of parenting three kids in three different seasons. "I'm not sure what we're doing tomorrow" didn't necessarily satisfy my extroverted son, but the white space it created on my calendar and in my soul helped me slow down and soak in that summer. My youngest who wasn't quite two stole naps when she could, often in the minivan, and reminded me she wouldn't be that little for long.

Lingering longer went against everything in my natural self that tends to want to be efficient and productive, but it always helped restore hope and joy to my soul. I'm a high-capacity person who multitasks pretty well, but lingering slowed my natural ways and kept what matters most at the forefront of my mind.

The idea about lingering longer is something I've held onto since reading *The Happiness Dare* by Jennifer Dukes Lee, but it took up residence in my life that summer, and hopefully will many more days to come regardless of the season. I love what Lee said about lingering:

"Science tells us when we linger longer—even for a few extra seconds—we are actually helping rewire our brains. Lingering helps our brains transfer positive feelings from our short-term memories into our long-term memories."[12]

I lingered in the grocery, where I've crossed paths with friends I don't see often enough. Hello, small-town living!

I lingered in the minivan as I finish texts to the people with whom I have ongoing conversations.

I lingered on the couch with my oldest when everyone else was sleeping or working, in the twin bed at bedtime with my middle, and on the floor with my youngest who discovers new details every day.

I lingered so much that all those projects I wanted to do that summer became ones I hoped to do in the fall and winter.

I lingered because the pace of this life is faster than I really want.

I lingered because I want to remember.

I lingered because these everyday moments matter in the big picture.

The lesson lasted beyond that one summer. Lingering longer is one way I've since created space to take care of myself. Yes, hospitality usually involves other people, but healing is a necessary part of anyone's life.

The summer after my dad unexpectedly died wasn't like other summers. Grief met me regularly during unexpected moments and prompted me to draw a smaller circle. I didn't invite many people over because being honest about how I was doing was difficult. Retelling the story of dad's death, the wounds it re-opened, and the secrets it revealed was exhausting. And not everyone truly understood the depths of my complicated grief.

Grieving during my favorite season was another layer of grief. I had to learn the hard way that sometimes summer is meant to be a time our souls can heal from a harsh winter, but I didn't like how my emotional winter was happening when the calendar and weather were really summer.

In counseling around that time, my counselor told me I was doing a good job taking care of myself. Honestly, doing so took a lot of effort because taking care of me meant pulling back from commitments on my calendar even when they involved people I enjoy being around. I had to let go of a regular commitment and say no to some invitations. I had to realize that my time at home didn't always have to be filled with productivity.

My friends are my favorites, but that season of grieving and healing was a time of drawing inward first and then going outward. I didn't have the energy to invest in relationships, so that summer only included my few closest friends and whoever invited me into their life. Becoming a better me meant I didn't initiate as many plans with friends, which meant I didn't see some friends as much because I'm usually the initiator. That brought more grief yet also led to more healing. Life can be tricky that way.

I'm barely an extrovert, enough that I like making new friends, want to hold onto them all forever, and generally create the community I crave. But everything in life has seasons, which is a hard but refreshing reality. Even though I felt like a different version of myself, I remained grateful for my friends—the ones who knew to check on me, the ones who I can pick up with when we do cross paths, the ones who have kids for my kids to befriend, and the ones I miss.

One day during that summer I was grieving, I woke up with no plan for the day. While that goes against my natural personality, I found the beauty of freedom in the wide-open space. And it was a good day—one with a healthy mixture of productivity and rest. I let my son choose a lunch spot and pick out new shoes. I said yes to exploring a creek bed that was a little outside my comfort zone. And I finished reading a book that spoke straight to my weary soul.

Author Kristen Strong didn't know she'd written a book that would be my companion that summer, but her words on belonging helped me navigate the social shift that happened in my grieving. *Back Roads to Belonging* was a gift to me. "When you believe you're in a season of wandering around a barren belonging landscape, may you know you don't wander purposelessly. God is aware of every bump and bend, and Jesus walks with you through every setback and delay. May you never stop participating in your own life, even through the mystery—because God is moving for you in your life. May you remember Jesus was brought outside so you could be brought inside forever."[13]

With a smaller circle, I found fresh perspective in belonging right where I am. The paths through the woods and the logging road that cuts through our country property were places I wandered freely as I wondered how I was going to step out of grief. I would make some progress, and then I'd feel the weight of other people's decisions, burdens I couldn't carry even if I wanted to, and the fact that life doesn't stop for grief.

One of the gifts that summer was a Bible study on Hebrews my friend Megan hosted and led. Honestly, I usually shy away from regular commitments in the summer, but I knew when she asked me about it in the spring that I wanted to go. I didn't anticipate backing off from some of my usual invitations. I didn't realize sorrow could lead to feelings of not belonging. I didn't know at the time I would need for someone to welcome me in.

Another gift that summer was my friendship with Becky. We'd known each other in passing for years. While I was grieving my dad's death and my sense of belonging, Becky was walking through her own grief prompted by some changes in her life. One change led to some other changes, and she and her family actually ended up moving at the end of that summer. But before they moved, Becky, her husband, and their two sons briefly attended our church. I didn't see all our conversations and time around tables coming, but God knew. He knew I needed her wisdom and authenticity. He knew she needed to belong in a different way too. He knew things we haven't even learned yet because that's how He provides and sustains us in our eternal belonging.

God kept the beauty and adventure right in front of me. He filled my soul when I felt empty. He reminded me of His promises for me and my place with Him. I was grateful then and am still today for my back roads and the belonging that happened when I lingered in my smaller circle.

STORY OF SHARED LIFE
EMILIE REINHARDT

Being in each other's lives is one of the ways God shows up in our lives on a monthly, weekly, and daily basis. I've never felt God so close and personal in my life as I have the first few months of my thirtieth year. I kicked off my new decade with a seven-and-a-half hour surgery that reconstructed my back. It was terrible but necessary. But what that necessary surgery also meant was that this single, thirty-year-old woman who could define the term "independent living" was suddenly very dependent on a lot of people. It was a necessary dependence, as necessary as the surgery was.

Rewind six months to this conversation and the following words I said: "My greatest fear with this surgery is not that I could wake up paralyzed, but that no one will be there to help me on the flip side. I've been there for so many people, and I'm scared I'll be forgotten, and no one will show up."

So what happened? The goodness of God showed up. I had 24/7 care from my friends and family, in fact, more so from my friends than my family. Friends showed up at 5:55 a.m. to relieve my housemate from her overnight shift and stayed until 10 or even 11 at night. Friends held the puke bowl for me when the medications disagreed with my body. Friends helped me get dressed, clipped my toe nails, put my socks on, and tied my shoes. Friends waited patiently in the bathroom and hand me my towel when I was done bathing. Friends brushed and braided my hair. Friends cleaned my house, changed my sheets, and did my laundry. Friends made meals for me for more than twelve weeks.

It took about three weeks for me to finally start letting go of control and start seeing what was happening. It was love on display. But it wasn't just the love my friends and family had for me; it was the love of Jesus that compelled them to show up. Just like the paralyzed man had his friends lower him to Jesus through a roof, so my friends brought me to the feet of Jesus, every single day.

That goodness of God that showed up, the love of God that showed up, was found in the people who cared, 24/7 for me, the food brought, Emily, Corrie, my insurance, Bill Call, my cell group, the mild and warm weather for winter we are having that lets me visit Socks almost every week, Nali, Dee Pavlack, Karen Trigg, Spotify music, my parents, Christian Community Church, Freeman's gift, texts with Kathy Koch, my brother Caleb, the new chair Caleb got me for my office, Kate and Jim, games of Splendor, Monica unpacking my house before surgery, Moe at the ICU, Marsha Adams, my sister chats, my Salomon shoes, safe commuting trips to and from work, cards from Gretchen Roe, all my friends, the hard conversations with Cara, Dr. O'Shaughnessy.

Those names may not mean a lot to anyone else, and those items may seem confusing to some, but that is the goodness of God showing up, through people, through community, and loving me, because of the power and love of Christ.

Emilie Reinhardt *is the definition of an ESFP and an enneagram 7 through and through. On any given day you can find her in the woods, on a mountain, playing with one of her dogs, babysitting one of her hooligans (nieces and nephews) or galloping around on her horse.*

Fall

Life is found in community with the Creator. Then there is God's call not only to live in self-sacrificing love of your neighbor, but also to be a tool of God's work in our neighbors' heart and life. You and I just don't have a choice of opting out. We are relational beings who have been called to lifelong community with God and others.

Paul David Tripp in *New Morning Mercies*

HOSPITALITY CONNECTS

Katie moved next door to me in October of 1990 and my life hasn't been the same since. She befriended the school principal's daughter and I was happy to have a new kid in the neighborhood. We didn't realize we were building a lifelong friendship. At the time, we ate Circus Peanuts, drank Dr Pepper, joked about fruitcake, and consumed more than our share of Hometown Pizza and Dairy Queen Blizzards.

When we met, she was 10 and I was 11. Now we're grown-ups who do frequent grocery shopping for our own families at two Kroger stores that are too far away from each other.

One time Katie sent me a card—yes, we sometimes still use the Postal Service to communicate—that says, "Sometimes I'll think about something you said, and I'll laugh, and then other people choosing tomatoes at the grocery store will wonder what's so funny about that tomato. (Open card.) You're good for me." And I laughed. Out loud. More than once. That's how we are. We really are good for each other and nobody thinks I'm funnier than Katie does.

Strangely but sweetly enough, my husband is distantly related to Katie, thanks to their common roots in a very small western Kentucky town. He once described us once as friends who make each other laugh at things nobody else would think are funny. We have inside jokes that drag on for decades, sometimes to the point we don't remember their origin or point. But we still laugh. And even though we haven't lived in the same town for more than half our friendship, I still know she'd rather have a short grocery list with so few items she can carry them all with a handheld basket, certainly without a cart. Just picturing her juggling a carton of orange juice, a gallon of milk, and cartons of ice cream makes me laugh.

In the fifteen months I was a mom before she was, I told her

more than once how when she had a child, juggling these items
wouldn't be possible—regardless of how strong and crafty she was.
That baby probably will weigh about eight pounds from the beginning. Add in the weight of the baby carrier moms inevitably have to
carry into the store because their babies fall asleep on the shortest of
drives. And, well, the orange juice and ice cream just have to find a
home in the cart.

She learned, like all us moms do about something. She now
mothers two boys and manages to keep them fed.

Through all the seasons, Katie has been in my life, even if many
miles have separated us almost all of our adult lives. Grown-up life
sure has its obstacles but they're easier to navigate with friends by
our side—wherever they live.

Here are some simple, practical ways to stay connected and
close the distance that physically separates loved ones:

1. Use social media to spark real conversations.
   Conversations may happen in emails, text messages,
   phone calls or Facebook messages, but they go deeper
   than what's happening on a public profile. Ask questions,
   swap stories, or continue previous conversations on a
   personal level. Maintaining long-distance friendships is
   certainly aided greatly by technology, but you still have to
   make an investment.
2. Send care packages and real mail. Yes, do it for birthdays
   or other special dates. But also do it just because.
3. Invite them over. Long-distance friends may not be
   conveniently located in your same town, but you can still
   invite them over. Get dates on the calendar and make
   plans. Another Katie in my life has become a faithful
   summer visitor to our house. In the winter, we make
   summer plans by setting aside a weekend for our families
   to spend together.
4. Be willing to go see them. When we go on a road trip,
   often prompted by a particular event, I try to schedule
   dates with other friends who live in that area. It doesn't

mean I can always see everyone I hope to see, but it's worth trying to connect over a meal.

5. Tell your kids about these friends. My kids adore some of my out-of-town friends. So when we do get to see them, they're just as excited as I am. Seeing my kids befriend my long-time friends' kids who live other places is one of the greatest joys of motherhood. And they adore the grown-up friends too when they know they're like family.

6. If you can't be there physically, send something. When my father-in-law passed away unexpectedly a decade ago, some out-of-town friends journeyed to our small town to grieve our loss and celebrate his life with us. Others couldn't be here, which is understandable, but they sent flowers, pictures frames, cards, and texts of prayers. Celebrate happier moments together across the miles too.

Yes, I'd love to be neighbors with Katie again, but that's not likely to happen, so we'll cherish the time we get to sit close on the couch and then continue connecting as we can to build upon our much-valued history.

STORY OF SHARED LIFE
CHRISTEN PRICE

Since the phrase social distancing surfaced in March 2020, my family and I were like the rest of the world during the coronavirus epidemic, adjusting to this new life of separation from others. We have all determined the one thing we missed most about our old routines was the times we spent in community with others. We missed our friends. We missed our family. We missed doing what we love, like small group, choir, and t-ball, with other people who loved doing those things too. Distancing ourselves from others was mandatory, so how did we find community and connection?

Hospitality connects us to one another when we are together, but hospitality also connects us to our people when we are apart. Connection is defined as "a relationship in which a person, thing, or idea is linked or associated with something else."[14] We were made for relationships with God and others. The time of social distancing was an opportunity for us to connect with the relationships we valued most. Here were three creative ways we stayed connected with our people while practicing social distancing:

1. **Car Caravans.** A friend recently turned eight and couldn't have a birthday party. So what did we do? We all made "Happy Birthday" signs and hopped in our cars to caravan to her house. We had a parade of people driving through her circular drive singing happy birthday and her mother said it was the best gift to her precious eight-year-old heart.

2. **Comfort Food.** A couple in our small group both work in the medical field as a doctor and a nurse. They informed us of the risks of the virus and were on the front lines wearing masks while treating patients as they enter the hospital. When they got home, all they desired was a hot shower and comfort food to ease them of their

daily anxiety. Our small group rotated dropping meals for them at their back door. We never saw them, but this little taste of hospitality let them know they weren't alone in the work they were doing.

3. **Computer Chats**. My closest group of girlfriends set up Zoom meetings once a week just so we could see one another's faces. We met in the evenings and we laughed, prayed, and talked about the serious and the silly. While nothing compares to physically being in the same room together, I'm reminded that we can stay connected even when we are apart.

Hospitality is love and love can extend itself through computer screens, caravans of cars, and comfort food. There are no limitations for love and it is during this time that I'm reminded how wide and long and high and deep the love of Christ is for each of us. He will meet us where we are and show us His hospitable love through the connections we have with our people. Let this time of distance draw us closer to people we love.

Christen Price lives in Alabama and is the author of "Invited: Life a Life of Connection, not Perfection." Connect with her at christenprice.com or @christenpricestudio.

HOSPITALITY SERVES

On my first-ever mission trip, I cried at dinner after our first day of work in Chichicastenango, Guatemala. A mixture of emotions collided in my head. I was missing Ben, who was back in the United States spending the week being spoiled by his grandmas. I was overwhelmed by the poverty I had already seen up close and feeling useless after spending the day at the site for a house build. The guys did all the hard work hand mixing concrete and pouring it as the foundation of a house we'd build the next day while Cate and I struggled to communicate with the family. Plus, I was in a third-world country with my then-eight-year-old daughter who was trying to process emotions of her own.

Our team leader Kim, who has since become a dear friend, gave me a pep talk when we stepped away from the table as everyone else was ordering their dinner. She reminded me God called us to this country, on this trip, at this time. Perhaps my broken Spanish, smiles, coloring books, and pieces of gum really did help that momma and her two kids feel loved while the guys poured concrete. Maybe I just needed to be a mom and help my girl try to grasp this new perspective in front of us.

Two Guatemalan kids—eleven-year-old Angelica and twelve-year-old Sergio—had the best smiles that day. Our broken Spanish made them laugh as they kept an eye on the concrete that would become the foundation of their house. And I stood there that evening in their homeland, crying.

As our team processed the day during our nightly devotional, we talked about foundations—the literal ones we were building and the spiritual one on which we build our faith. This family was going from having a dirt floor beneath their adobe house to a metal house built upon a concrete slab. Talk about security and improvement.

But sometimes security in Christ comes when we step out of our comfort zone.

That's what happened for me in Guatemala that week in 2015. I eventually dried my tears and decided to let God use me—even if that didn't look like I expected, even when that made my heart race, even when I wasn't sure what He would do with the seeds we were planting with our service, prayers, and hugs. With Jesus as the foundation, we can have hope and assurance there's goodness to come.

We saw Angelica and Sergio the next afternoon when we went to build their house. And two days later Angelica was at another home we were building just down the dirt road and through the cornfields from her new house. When we walked up to build that second home, Angelica looked at me and said "Hola!" like we were friends. There was still a language barrier, but we had bonded anyway. And now we had a chance to serve Maria and her four kids, including nine-year-old Brenda. I gave Angelica, Maria, and Brenda a bag of embroidery thread. Cate joined them to make friendship bracelets—joining in with much more ease than that first day.

These Guatemalans made us beautiful bracelets far superior to our braided ones. Then Maria turned the hacky sack she was crocheting into a pouch for Cate. Yes, it was beautiful and created in love. But it was also a sacrifice because she could have sold the hacky sack at the local market for money for her family. Instead she chose to give it to my girl. We were there serving them, yet we were blessed.

I carried supplies, used a drill, helped hold a wall, and assembled bunk beds that day. I watched a team of people come together and build a house—and relationships with each other. But my favorite moment of the day came when women and girls used thread to make gifts and tie together sweet memories.

That week in Guatemala changed me. Yes, the poverty I saw makes me thankful for my life and all the many opportunities here. But it also reminds me people everywhere have needs. I saw God in a new way there—and I want to keep my eyes open to seeing Him that way wherever I am.

God led us back to Guatemala three years later—this time with my boy Ben joining us. He was about the same age as Cate when we first went. Leaving Rachel was hard this time, but I knew the four of us were supposed to go. In almost every way, having Ben with us was easier than I expected. He bravely connected with other kids with whom he didn't share a language, sharing suckers and gum and toy cars and LEGO blocks. We loved seeing him bond with one of the ministry workers and one of the sons of another missionary.

He managed to fall into a swimming pool without water on our last night there, but we were relieved that miraculously it wasn't as bad an injury as it initially looked and that he didn't fall down the mountain where he chased chickens earlier in the week. Really, living with Ben shows me ordinary miracles regularly. He's spunky and adventurous. He's brave and curious. He's sweet and remembers more than anyone thinks he does. He finds joy in everyday moments. His strengths are my weaknesses. God uses my boy for my good and the good of many around him.

That's why I wanted to take him to Guatemala. Plus, we believe in serving as a family, so as a family we go wherever God leads us.

Of course, that second trip to Guatemala shifted my perspective again.

We met a family with five kids—two girls who were in their 20s and their three much younger brothers. When we visited, the seventy-one-year-old dad and forty-nine-year-old mom were working in nearby fields. The girls told us about how they didn't get to go to school when they were younger, so they still lived at home to help provide enough money so their brothers could go to school. Going to school costs money because there are required supplies and uniforms, but often families have to choose between education and food.

These two twenty-something-year-old girls didn't want their parents to have to sacrifice their brothers' education. So they waited to be married and start families of their own. They take care of the two-room house with a dirt floor. They weave beautiful belts other women in this culture with Mayan roots love.

They make intentional sacrifices for the well-being of others. That's how hospitality serves.

Just down the road in this little community of Paquip, we met a dad of twelve kids. His wife was working in the fields. Some of the other kids were doing other jobs to support each other. The oldest daughter at home that afternoon told us about how she sings in area churches, who give her offerings that help buy corn to make tortillas and black beans for protein.

Again, she could be pursuing her own life, but she's pouring into her family so her siblings can have opportunities too. In fact, one of her younger brothers is twelve years old and hadn't planned on continuing beyond sixth grade next year because the price of education doubles then. Our team was able to secure an education sponsor for this boy, who wants to be a teacher.

Intentional sacrifices.

During the week in and around Tecpan, Guatemala, our team visited eighteen other families and found ways to help most of them, distributed fifty-one wheelchairs, poured two concrete slabs for houses after mixing it by hand and then built metal houses on them later in the week, and installed eight stoves. We did all this alongside missionaries Hannah and Saul who work full time with Bethel Ministries International—a ministry Hannah's parents started decades ago. Pastor Juan and his wife Anna serve in this area of Guatemala and helped Bethel find people who needed physical assistance. Their son David helps with the construction projects and was easy to work with. Saul's brother Marvin does various jobs with Bethel and was a joy to be around. There are others who work and serve with this ministry we've come to trust and respect.

More intentional sacrifices. That's the kind of hospitality that Jesus wants us to show others because in serving we're actually honoring Him. What we do for others, especially the least of these, is what we do to Jesus (Matt. 25:31-40). This is how we're supposed to live—wherever we are, with whatever our skill set, and alongside whoever we meet. God has shown His faithfulness as He's provided what we don't always realize we need. As our faith grows, we are able to love and serve others—not just for a week in Guatemala but all the days of our regular lives.

Yes, that lifestyle takes some intentional sacrifices of our time and money and comforts, but it pales in comparison to the one God made with His son on a cross for our sake. Let's imitate intentional sacrifice and rejoice for the opportunities and beauty doing so brings.

STORY OF SHARED LIFE
KATIE MITCHELL

In church I used to hear sermons about spiritual gifts and would wonder what mine was. It took those closest to me and the Bible study *Rooted* to reveal that my gift is hospitality. Hospitality (especially in the South which I will claim since I was born in Memphis and I love hugs) means a warm and welcoming invitation into your home.

I grew up in a home where hosting seasonal parties was the norm—Christmas parties for my dad's employees; spring teas on the front porch for the church ladies; summer cookouts for my youth group. Whatever it was, my parents always seemed to host the perfect party—the food, the decorations, the games, the prizes. Everything was carefully thought out and executed. But even as a kid, I noticed how much effort and work went in to hosting those "perfect" events.

As I went on to build my own life, and then literally our own home, I wanted our space to be one that welcomed people in with love and comfort, and of course I too wanted to host fun parties just as my parents had done throughout my childhood. I'm happy to say we've done just that, having Christmas parties for friends, even incorporating the crazy dice game my family once played years ago at those company events. We've hosted the families of our son's baseball team for food and fun in the backyard. We've held neighborhood gatherings for both business and fellowship too. We've hosted our small group countless times (ten adults and twice as many kids!), sitting now on our own front porch to share discussion that is sometimes funny, sometimes hard, but always life-giving.

As I reflect on all this, I think, "Wow, we've had some amazing times with people in this home!" But, if I'm being honest, the perfectionist in me has felt internally stressed prior to and during each get-together. I worry about everyone liking the food. Do they think the game is fun? Are they enjoying themselves? This unfortunately often means I'm not fully present in the moment. I care what others think about me and what I put out there to the world. Therefore, I can really get in my head about everything being successful.

One thing I'm learning through the grace and love of genuine friends is these gatherings don't have to be perfect. If you burn the cornbread that was supposed to be the perfect addition to your best-ever chili, it's okay. If you totally forget one of the sides you were going to make and run out of food to feed everyone, it's okay. If the internet is down and the playlist you made to be the perfect soundtrack to your party can no longer be heard, it's okay. In the end, whether we've gathered to share a meal, play a game, or throw a ball in the backyard, these are all moments in which God is calling me to be present and lean in. It's not about the perfect party. It's about loving others well. I am slowly changing, trying to take the best of what I learned about hospitality growing up and molding that through the lens of Jesus into a home that is inviting but not pretentious, welcoming but not perfect.

Katie Mitchell lives in southern Indiana with her husband, Aaron, who she met through the author, and their boys, Ben, Will, and Wes; works as an oncology/hematology nurse practitioner; and is known for her laugh and her "best-ever" recommendations.

Hospitality Grieves

The way we grieve changes when we have kids.

When Cate was three, she had lots of questions. Truthfully, since she started talking, she's had questions. But back then she mostly had two questions that can be applied to many, many situations: "Why, momma?" And this girl has obviously seen me plan our days: "Where are we goin'?"

She knows I'll have an answer. I always do.

One day, when I loaded Cate and her eight-month-old brother into the new-to-us minivan that makes running errands so much more pleasant, I thought I might prevent the toddler version of Twenty Questions. I told her we were going to run an errand.

"We goin' to the blue store?" she asks, referring to the blue font on the front of Kroger, where we do our weekly grocery shopping.

"No, we're going to another store." Again, too general.

"Oh, we goin' to the yellow store," she assumes, referring to Walmart's yellowish brick building that sits across the street from Kroger.

"Actually, no. We're going to Rite-Aid," I said.

No more questions for the moment. She was content being included in the plan.

Then from the back seat she randomly brought up her Granddaddy, who passed away suddenly almost four months earlier. He died of a heart attack a month before Cate turned three. Trying to help her make sense of his sudden departure, we had previously explained that his heart stopped working. The night Daddy told his always-thinking daughter about Granddaddy's heart, she instantly suggested we get some new batteries. Oh, sweet girl, if life were only that simple.

We also tried to explain that Granddaddy is living with Jesus. One day we'll join him, but he's not coming back here. Death—even when it means living eternally in heaven—is a hard concept to grasp for anyone, especially for a girl who adored her Granddaddy. I've learned even little ones have coping strategies, and Cate's was apparently to talk about it. Who knows what prompted her to think about him at that moment on the way to the pharmacy. But she did. So we talked.

Of course, she began with a question: "Remember Granddaddy's heart stopped working and he's living with Jesus?"

It was bittersweet then and it's bittersweet now. I'm glad she listened to our too-early lesson on heaven, but I'm sad she didn't get to know Granddaddy better. "Yes. I miss Granddaddy. I know you do too."

Her mind was still working. I could tell, even though she was sitting directly behind me and I couldn't see her face without glancing in my rear-view mirror. "When my heart stops working, I will go live with Granddaddy and Jesus. Tomorrow I will."

"Probably not tomorrow. But one day. One day we'll go live with Jesus and Granddaddy."

Again, bittersweet. I couldn't bear the thought of Cate not being with us, but I adored the way she adored the man she missed.

"We can get Granddaddy batteries, so he come here with me," she said, returning to her original solution.

"Granddaddy will be with Jesus forever. We'll join them one day."

And she returned to the questions: "When?"

"When God decides our time here in this life is finished."

I wasn't sure if the questions ended there because she was satisfied or baffled, but I looked into her eyes with a glance into my rear-view mirror and knew what Jesus meant when he encouraged people to have childlike faith.

Sorrow over losing my father-in-law and my own father a decade later taught me about Jesus and heaven. The gospel is ultimately about death, burial, and resurrection. There's so much promise in that, but there is sorrow too. They can co-exist and Jesus can restore what is broken into something beautiful because He makes a way for sorrow to end.

I want to live with heaven in mind—especially as a mom.

I think of heaven when I hear my Kenyan friend Daniel pray. I remember heaven when I remember the prayers in Spanish when we blessed the home we built for a family near Tecpan, Guatemala on a mission trip. I am drawn to worship music that lets me hear accents of people's homeland, whether that's Ireland or Georgia.

All the tongues, even the ones I can't understand with my American ears, are praising the same God, the one who sent His son for us. Jesus has gone to prepare a place for us, and the tapestry of voices is going to be beautiful when we get there, just like Revelation 7:9-12 says:

"After this I looked, and behold, a great multitude that no one could number, from every nation, from all tribes and peoples and languages, standing before the throne and before the Lamb, clothed in white robes, with palm branches in their hands, and crying out with a loud voice, 'Salvation belongs to our God who sits on the throne, and to the Lamb!' And all the angels were standing around the throne and around the elders and the four living creatures, and they fell on their faces before the throne and worshiped God, saying, 'Amen! Blessing and glory and wisdom and thanksgiving and honor and power and might be to our God forever and ever! Amen.'"

But we aren't there yet. Sorrow still lives here too—and sometimes that's hard to understand. Only heaven can give us perspective to keep going here, like Paul David Tripp writes: "The fact is that you cannot make sense out of life unless you look at it from the vantage point of eternity. If all God's grace gives us is a little better here and now, if it doesn't finally fix all that sin had broken, then perhaps we have believed in vain. . . . There has to be more to God's plan than this world of sin, sickness, sorrow, and death. There has to be more than the temporary pleasures of this physical world. Yes, there is more, and when you live like there's more to come, you live in a radically different way."[15]

As I shuttle kids around and navigate all the conversations required, I don't think about heaven as much as I should. I think about what it's like to live here in our self-absorbed culture, how I should best raise my kids to be believers here, and whether I'm doing enough to point them to Jesus. But I don't parent with heaven in mind.

I want to change that. I want to point my kids to Jesus because He's preparing a place for them too, not just because His example is the right way to live here in our temporary homes. I want to teach them about living with an eternal perspective because so few things truly matter like we think they do. I want to love and learn alongside them. I want to live with a gaze toward heaven, where all the tribes and nations will be one. I'm guessing I'll understand those prayers from the Guatemalans, and forget about sorrow when we get there.

STORY OF SHARED LIFE
LESLIE CATES

My husband and I were moving into a carriage house apartment above our dear friends' garage. They graciously offered to rent it to us for a song, because I was pregnant, and we were having trouble making ends meet. Living in a large city away from home, their friendship was a blessing to us from the moment we were introduced, and they quickly became like family. We shared a love for cooking and eating good food, so coming around a table for delicious meals was how we connected throughout the week. They rejoiced with us as we announced my pregnancy, which is always a time to rejoice. Even more so, since I had been infertile for many years, this baby was a miracle from God! We began to move in the carriage house, and I was excited to finally be able to set up that baby crib I had waited so long for.

The week we were moving, I went to a routine doctor's visit, and it was discovered that our baby's heart had stopped beating. At 16 weeks along, I was experiencing my worst nightmare! The days following were mostly a blur. While we were in the hospital, our parents came to support us and moved everything, and even unpacked for us so I could recover. Once our family left, after the graveside ceremony we had on that beautiful early August day, the loneliness and deep sadness really creeped in. I missed my parents, and I mourned our baby, so I spent my time inside just wanting to recover from all that had happened—the miscarriage, the delivery, the burial, the move. Everything felt "off."

My dear friend who lived in the home beneath ours called the night following the burial and asked if I wanted to come down to their screened-in porch. I resisted a visit so soon. I was wrapped up in sorrow I didn't want to let go of! How could I enjoy anything yet? I couldn't go down after being a ball of tears for the last week. I was tired and the couch felt good. My husband knew in that moment that the invitation for me to go down for some girl-time was a God-

ordained moment. I didn't see it that way—not yet. However, I listened to his nudge, and I slipped on my flip-flops and met my friend on her porch.

She greeted me as she always does with a smile and her peaceful presence. She didn't overwhelm me with words, for she was acquainted with the deep loss of a loved one herself. I sat down on the rattan chair with the overhead fan spinning away on that hot evening, and she brought to me a beautiful tray with delicate plates carrying slices of homemade chocolate cake. Next to the cake there were lovely cups of rich, dark roast coffee with a small pitcher of cream. While pregnant I didn't drink coffee, so accepting that cup she offered felt like a brave step I needed to take toward healing. My friend sat with me as I put into words the whole experience from the previous week. Her presence beside me as I slowly indulged in the delicious cake and sipped steaming coffee with her allowed me to just be. I remember taking a deep breath for the first time in a long time, and in that moment, I could feel God tell me: Enjoy this moment as a gift!

My dear friend's invitation was a gift. A gift I didn't know that I needed that very evening, and one I was ready to decline. Thank goodness she didn't allow the depressing circumstances to stop her from calling me. I didn't let my dirty hair and grave demeanor keep me away when I got her invitation—the invitation to truly "taste and see that the Lord is good" (Psalm 34:8). That night as we sat on her screened in porch, sharing chocolate cake, and salty tears, a seed of healing was planted, and that was when I understood the true meaning of hospitality.

Leslie Cates is a happy wife, a worship leader, and a coffee-loving stay-at-home mom raising three kids she was blessed with through the miracle of adoption.

HOSPITALITY WELCOMES

The grocery stores in our small town feel different when the college students return. The same fall day my big kids went to second and fifth grades, I went to the grocery. I was silently celebrating my own back-to-school-week grocery shopping trip as I bought the baby carrots, Wheat Thins, yet another gallon of milk, bread, eggs, not-yet-ripe bananas along with one already spotting that would be good for banana bread sooner rather than later, mini Oreos, and four kinds of cheese.

Then I saw four college boys who were obviously doing their own kind of back-to-school shopping. Dressed in khakis, collared shirts, and flip flops as if the friendships came with a dress code, they walked together into the dairy section. One wandered to the eggs and said to his friends lingering in the frozen foods, "How many eggs do we need?" One of his friends advised him to get one carton of 12 eggs, so he did.

I really wanted to explain to him that my family of five—that includes no college-aged boys—eats at least eight eggs at one time. Surely these boys—perhaps they'd prefer "men"—need more than a dozen eggs. Won't they make all those for one breakfast? Do college guys even eat breakfast together? Honestly, I wouldn't have thought they'd shop together, so I'm clearly not the one to ask.

As I'm having these conversations in my own head, I hear another one of the college guys say, "Hey, did anyone get the salsa?" Priorities, obviously. They did have that in the cart. Then they nego-tiated how they'd pay for the cart-load. Yes, once again, I wanted to offer advice: Just go pay for it and then when they get home split up the total. I wanted to mother these boys-almost-men.

Our town changes when the students come back each August. The traffic is heavier, the restaurants busier, and the grocery store aisles slightly more entertaining. And I like it.

This college town is my college town and now it's my hometown. Murray State is where I met my husband and grew up as a person. Our best friends are college friends. College memories collide with my everyday life because I often drive by where my dorm used to be before they tore it down. This is where I'm raising my kids as people and Racer fans.

Individually and through our church, we still support the campus ministry that helped influence us for the good while we were earning our bachelor's degrees and gave us some great friends. My family has made a couple new college-aged friends because of this same campus ministry and we still miss the former-student-now-adult who was our go-to babysitter for several years.

So, welcome back to Murray, college kids. I'm glad you want to be in our town. It's a good place to call home. And, hey, my family is here if you need any grocery shopping tips or want a home-cooked meal.

When Amber was still a college student, she was comfortable enough at our house that she tapped on the back door and then just walked in. I greeted her from the kitchen and my kids literally jumped on her and her then-boyfriend, now-husband. She was my kids' babysitter and now we're all still friends.

Amber had previously asked me if she and Sean could meet with us regularly and just talk. For college students, they were being wise as they pursued their relationship with each other. Greg and I have an imperfect story we are happy to share. We like where we are, even though most parts of our life are nothing like I planned. We started dating in college, like Amber and Sean. We were all involved in the same campus ministry—albeit more than a decade apart. We studied different things and I never ever had or will ever have a pet snake like she has. We're glad they're in our lives. Yes, reminiscing with them makes us feel old sometimes, but we like opening our life to them. Our kids adore them. And there are only a couple of people who have always understood my boy as well as Amber does.

One day they came over for dinner. It had been a full day, but all of us were excited to see them. I made extra food for a friend while watching an extra kid and prepared to have Amber and Sean over for dinner. I was still potty training my boy while parenting a kindergartener who liked to talk.

It wasn't a bad day. In fact, most of it was smooth and good. But the real-life chaos caught up with me in the four o'clock hour as I made dinner. So when Amber walked in my kitchen and asked "How's your day been?" all that I could come up with was "tiring." As I was saying it, I realized my response made me sound ungrateful for these little people who fill my house and the opportunities to spend time with and help my friends. I knew as I was classifying my day as tiring, there are people who work harder and longer than I do every day of their lives without the conveniences I have. I wanted my husband to come home. And when he did, I felt like I would crumble out of relief of no longer being the only one in charge. He tried to help. I got snippy and demanding. We all sat down at the table and I still wanted to cry. I felt every whine, request, and disobedience from the whole day—both mine and the kids'—catching up with me. Frustrations filled my heart.

My perspective improved over dinner. Just sitting and having other adults around helped. Amber helped me clean up the table. We played with the kids for a while. Then the little ones went to bed, our guests left, I washed some dishes, packed the kids' lunches for the next day, and eventually sat down with two Reese's Cups that I'd picked up impulsively earlier in the day.

My husband and I got into bed early. We both were worn down from different kinds of busy days. I closed out a full day with words by author Holley Gerth that were good for my soul: "Oh, no, friends. God has more for you—so much more than you can even imagine. You are made in His image, and the more you display all that He has placed in you, the more you bring Him glory. And when we bring Him glory, we feel joy, freedom, and purpose. Life becomes a gift rather than a chore." [16]

Amen. Yes, my day was tiring. I felt weary. But that's not all there is. My day and life aren't limited to that because I have a purpose in these days of mothering and serving. Amber wanted to be mentored, and that evening was as real as it gets. It wasn't perfect, but it was part of the process God is using to draw my family to Him and show us and others the glory that outshines every other imperfect human emotion and response that we use to define our days.

We still share meals with Amber and Sean now that they're married and live four hours away. Ben still hugs her and she still encourages him. We helped at their wedding, meet for dinner when we're in the area, and text life updates to each other. We kick my daughter out of her room so they can have a bed when they come visit for Murray State's Homecoming each fall. I think I'll always be a little mothering toward Amber, both with the advice I have to give and the pride I feel as I watched her grow into adulthood so beautifully. Our friendship started when she was playing with some kids, including mine, at a church party and grew in lots of little moments that ended up being a profound blessing for us all.

Hospitality makes others feel at home when it happens in the midst of real life. This is where I want to live out my faith.

STORY OF SHARED LIFE
JACLYN Tompkins

Community is defined as a feeling of fellowship with others, as a result of sharing common attitudes, interests, and goals. As a teacher, community is very important to me. It is important to me to be part of the community that my students are in. It is important to make my classroom a community of learners who feel safe just being themselves. It is important that I work in a community of teachers where we are all on the same page. Much to my surprise, God opened the door for me to be part of the Symsonia community in 2016. I did not see that coming. That was not part of my plan. I had no idea where this small town was located. It's almost 30 miles from where I live. I did not know anyone there. But soon I became part of that community and it became part of me.

Community welcomes. I was unaware that I did actually know a teacher who worked at Symsonia Elementary. We had worked together before, and both share a love for reading and teaching reading. My new teaching partner welcomed me by answering the many, many questions I had about my new school—new expectations, new routines, new schedules, new programs, new content. As Back to School night approached, I dreaded the ceremony where the new teachers would be introduced in the gym in front of all the students and families. But as my principal announced my name, I heard some cheers from the principal's daughter and friends (who were assigned to my class!) welcoming me to their school. The next week when the first Spirit Day occurred, I found two new Symsonia T-shirts on my desk. Now I would match my fellow co-workers. I couldn't remember the last time I felt so welcome.

Community levels the playing field. As I spent weeks preparing my classroom to be a welcoming atmosphere for students, different colleagues came by and introduced themselves. One day it was the secretary. One day it was an instructional assistant. One day it was one of the lunch ladies. One day it was a fellow teacher. I'd never been in a school where the playing field was so level. Everyone mattered. Everyone's work mattered. And the bottom line was we do what's best for kids.

Community is safe. When everyone is on the same page and everyone matters, there is a sense of safety. And when an introvert like myself works for an extrovert like my principal, a sense of safety is vital. Safety is essential when she asked us to dress up like a pirate and film a "movie" complete with songs to show in the gym before testing. Or when she asked us to be part of a dance routine and lip sync contest in front of the school. Safety in community allows us to stretch. And although it's good to stretch when your boss asks you to, you begin to realize you can do things you didn't think you could. Like learning to play pickleball because the adorable seventy-year-old male nurse wants to play. I'd never subjected anyone to my lack of athleticism before, but here I felt safe enough to try.

Whether it's being part of a community or trying to create one yourself, everyone appreciates feeling welcome, being on a level playing field, and feeling safe.

Jaclyn Tompkins *is the daughter of the King, wife, momma of three, and teacher of many.*

Hospitality Supports

We all need people to come along side us to be successful—and sometimes that means letting it be known we need help.

There's nothing like a war story from the Old Testament to illustrate this point: "The Amalekites came and attacked the Israelites at Rephidim. Moses said to Joshua, 'Choose some of our men and go out to fight the Amalekites. Tomorrow I will stand on top of the hill with the staff of God in my hands.' So Joshua fought the Amalekites as Moses had ordered, and Moses, Aaron and Hur went to the top of the hill. As long as Moses held up his hands, the Israelites were winning, but whenever he lowered his hands, the Amalekites were winning. When Moses' hands grew tired, they took a stone and put it under him and he sat on it. Aaron and Hur held his hands up—one on one side, one on the other—so that his hands remained steady till sunset. So Joshua overcame the Amalekite army with the sword. Then the Lord said to Moses, 'Write this on a scroll as something to be remembered and make sure that Joshua hears it, because I will completely blot out the name of Amalek from under heaven.' Moses built an altar and called it The Lord is my Banner. He said, 'Because hands were lifted up against the throne of the Lord, the Lord will be at war against the Amalekites from generation to generation.'"[17]

Moses, Aaron, and Hur went up to the top of the hill so they could see and know how to pray. They were faithful to Joshua, who was faithful to them. Each positioned themselves to serve one another well. Then when Moses' hands were tired, Aaron and Hur helped him.

There are different ways to win the battle. Joshua fought. Moses prayed. Aaron and Hur helped. That victory over the Amalekites required all of them, was worth remembering, and ultimately belonged to God.

I've never been at war, but I've needed support plenty of times.

I have a full history of meaningful friendships, but sometimes schedules and moves and seasons leave me feeling lonely and without support. During one of these times, I felt on edge as I tried to navigate life alone. I missed friends who were easy to be around and knew all the back stories. I longed for deeper connections with people I saw regularly. I missed the summer that had just passed and found myself looking toward spring. I ended up crying and spewing all these feelings toward my husband. He listened and then said something simple yet profound, "Have you told your friends you're lonely?"

I hadn't told him or anyone I felt lonely. I hadn't reached out to friends. I hadn't let it be known my heart was tired like Moses' arms. And I found myself far from any emotional victory.

Asking for support is okay because it can be a step toward victory. I ended up talking to several friends about how I was feeling, and they were quick to come alongside me with support, encouragement, and advice.

Not long after I crashed and burned trying to do life all alone, my friend Courtney invited me to a ladies' night at her church. I put it on my calendar, which means I made a personal commitment to set aside time for that. Closer to time, I invited two other friends to go with me to this event from which I didn't even know what to expect. We laughed together about how we don't usually do anything social for ourselves on a school night. Through the message, music, and time together at a table, we remembered we weren't alone. We were reminded of the value of friendship and how it's always been an important element of stories, like Moses praying for his friend and army with his other friends by his side as support.

I've had to learn the friends who will be available to support us may change based on the season—and that's okay. Yes, I know, I have to give myself pep talks to remind myself change is okay, even when it's hard. But God will continue to provide what we need, including people in our lives. Of course, none of us are perfect. Hospitality is grace—for you and for me, like John Piper says:

"Grace is the hospitality of God to welcome sinners not because of their goodness but because of his glory."[18]

When my kids were little, I had a near-daily community of other moms around me. We were quick to gather. Our kids played and we connected. Honestly, friendship was pretty easy then. As our kids grew up, friendships became harder because we found ourselves immersed in different work schedules, different schooling schedules and choices, more taxi driving responsibilities to different practices and commitments, and varying parenting seasons. The differences sometimes seemed greater than our shared histories, but then several of us remembered the victories we'd shared. We could mark those and still figure out new ways to connect. This likely isn't the only time our kids growing up will force our ways of connecting to shift, but our God is faithful to us and we can be faithful support to one another—even when it might look different the next time.

STORY OF SHARED LIFE
MARy CARVER

Again I say to you, if two of you agree on earth about
anything they ask, it will be done for them by my Father
in heaven. For where two or three are gathered in my
name, there am I among them.

Matthew 18-19-20

My church encourages members to join small groups, believing that
life is better and faith is stronger when we live in community with
others. But it also values the growth and fellowship that can develop
in a one-on-one (or one-on-one-on-one) friendship. We call these
accountability groups "two-three groups," for no reason other than
they are made of two or three people.

I was part of a two-three group with two women from my small
group. As we met every week, discussing a chapter from the book we
were reading together and watching our children play together, our
friendships grew deeper, and we felt comfortable sharing our most
intimate stories and our most difficult challenges. The time we spent
together, talking and praying and laughing and crying, was a gift.

Though I knew one of my friends was struggling with a situation
in her life, I was surprised when she suddenly left town. Life had
become even more painful than she'd shared and, needing a safe
place to process and heal, she visited her family for a few weeks.
Our two-three group was down to two, and we weren't sure what to
do at first.

Thank God for technology though!

After a few days had passed and our regularly scheduled day to
meet came around, we decided we wouldn't let a few hundred miles
keep us apart. Two of us sat at the kitchen table, staring intently into
an iPad as if that screen could tell us if our friend was okay, truly
okay, and we talked to our sweet friend on the other side of the

screen. We talked and we cried and then, when we were—at least for then—out of words and tears, we prayed.

Distance couldn't stop us or God. Holding onto the tablet when we couldn't hold onto one another that day, we gathered in Jesus' name. United in spirit even as we sat in separate kitchens, we agreed and we asked and we went to God together.

__Mary Carver__ is a writer and speaker who loves finding (and sharing) Truth in unexpected places. Find her at marycarver.com.

Hospitality Loves

My college sweetheart husband and I do many things together, usually with our kids in tow. We go to Murray State football and basketball games. I've taught him Scrabble strategies so well he often beats me at the game I used to win. We like road trips and vacations. We believe weekends were meant to be spent as a family, but sometimes we go on dates to my favorite local fish restaurant near Kentucky Lake or road trip to Nashville for a concert together.

But we do not go grocery shopping together.

In our first year of marriage, I worked as a newspaper reporter and Greg was in his last year of law school. We spent our days doing our own things and then in the evenings we regularly did grown-up things, like grocery shop in a Kroger in Lexington, Kentucky. We usually ended up arguing before we paid for our groceries. Nothing like breaking in a new marriage while picking out apples. But it wasn't my choice in apples that irked him or his love of frozen pizza that frustrated me. We just had different grocery shopping strategies, and, well, we're both first-born children who are confident we know the best way to do pretty much everything. He wanted to divide up the grocery list I had made and tag team the shopping. Meanwhile, I wanted to start in the produce section, work our way by the deli, to the meat department, onto the canned food aisle, and eventually end up in the dairy section. Together. I wanted to scout deals, compare prices, ensure the right quantities were bought, and remain loyal to the brands I love yet, buy the Kroger brand of certain items.

Personality traits came into play here: My love language is quality time, so I figured grocery shopping together was time spent together, thus I felt loved. I much later recognized my natural personality and how I have my own rules about anything and every-thing, apparently even grocery shopping. Meanwhile, efficiency is always Greg's goal.

Despite my systematic approach to the grocery aisles, I didn't like cooking early in that first year of our marriage. Or the next four. I eventually decided cooking wasn't so bad, but I still don't bake. Thankfully, now our oldest daughter makes the best chocolate chip cookies. And Greg and I still don't grocery shop together. When I worked in the newsroom, I'd go after work before he got home. When I became a stay-at-home mom, I learned the beauty of grocery shopping in the morning, when the aisles are much less crowded and my kids were their best selves.

Truthfully, I'd rather take my kids with me than my husband. They've been trained. And they actually aren't the ones who throw Betty Crocker yellow cake mix and a tub of chocolate icing in the cart.

Thankfully, we quickly learned marriages are sometimes better off when we don't do every single thing together. I'm also grateful Greg and I do spend plenty of time together doing things—none of which include baking that cake mix he bought. Our marriage will be better if we concentrate on those activities and stay out of the grocery store when we do have time together.

In honor of an anniversary of our first date on February 14, 1998, I gave Greg one of those trendy personalized signs of family "rules." I wanted to celebrate the process that began when he asked me out for ice cream 14 years earlier and has continued into parenthood. Some seasons have been hard. Others have been downright ugly. But so many have been sweet and plenty have been adventurous. I mean, we literally jumped off a bridge together when we bungee jumped in New Zealand. It was exciting and daring and a once-in-a-lifetime kind of thing. That's just one of the big moments woven together with the many smaller moments that make our life.

Most days are ordinary. He goes to work. When the kids were little, I changed diapers and filled cups with milk and juice. We met friends at the park. He went to meetings for work, to serve on community boards, and to help lead our church. As the kids have gotten older, I have an efficient taxi service, keep a calendar of soccer practices and family events, and we still meet friends at the park sometimes. We invite others to share dinners I prepared now that I know how to cook and offer up stories of what God has done for us.

Regardless of what parenting season we're in, we almost always have dinner together. Thus "SIT DOWN for DINNER" is on our family rules that I gifted my husband and now hangs in our dining room in the center of our house. That "rule" could have been a reminder to my then-two-year-old son who liked to kneel and constantly move around in his chair during any meal, creating scattered crumbs like a trail of where he has been. It could also be a reminder to our now-four-year-old third child who is active, mischievous, and likes to entertain when anyone is watching. But the point of the "rule" is we believe our family is and will be stronger because we prioritize each other and the meals we share.

That's where hospitality begins, right here with the five of us, and then outward to a broader circle. On the nights two kids have soccer practice, Greg coaches one of them, and I'm keeping track of where everyone is, we might sit down for dinner together at Culver's, where we bribe everyone to eat their fried food so they can have ice cream too. On the nights I have a school board meeting, we might meet at Zaxby's for chicken someone else cooked and then move the booster seat and the kids to Greg's truck so they can go on home.

These meals aren't even about the food. They are about the time and conversations. We tell Daddy about our day, and he tells some about his. While talking about the ordinary moments Greg and I have fostered an environment where we (and our kids) stay bonded even when we our ankles aren't tied together so we can safely jump off a bridge. This bond helps us (usually) stay united while we make spiritual, financial, and parenting decisions that may challenge us. It also helps us enjoy each other and our kids as individuals.

I longed for a family and consider our team my favorite, but families can be complicated. As wife and mom, I often consider what is best for us collectively, but sometimes I accidentally overlook my people as individuals with their own preferences and personalities. I let outside stresses affect what's happening inside my family.

Then I remember how Jesus "is before all things, and in him all things hold together" (Colossians 1:17). Even so, remembering a truth and actually living there aren't the same thing. I'm thankful for new mercies and another chance to live like I really believe Christ holds us—as individuals and a unit—together.

Even with cornbread crumbs scattered across the floor and constant reminders to sit down until everyone is done, being around the table helps us connect in a world that is full of busy schedules and temptations to keep moving along at a pace that will eventually pull us apart.

So, yes, we sit down for dinner. We walk away filled, and not just from food because hospitality happens right where we are with our loved ones.

STORY OF SHARED LIFE
JAMIE MCKENZIE

As an eighteen-year-old I ended up on the doorstep of a small non-denominational church in our town. The church building wasn't anything ritzy or eye catching, but the community of believers it held was like a hidden jewel.

I know some of you can relate to what I'm saying. For whatever reason, God led you to a particular community. A community where you were welcomed, loved, embraced, and wanted. A community of givers, not takers. A community that looks like that of the early church in the book of Acts, and now that community has become your standard. So, I settled down here and made this community my home. I decided to unpack my bags and stay, and by doing so, I was unknowingly allowing God to deepen my understanding about sharing life and showing hospitality.

This community taught me that hospitality means you welcome people. Jesus says the whole law can be summed up in two commands: Love God and love your neighbor. Welcoming someone, either into your home or at your church or as you're out running errands, is such an easy way to communicate that love. When we are welcoming to people, we put them at ease and offer them a place in our lives. We are communicating to them that they have worth and value.

This community taught me God doesn't leave me high and dry. He uses community to bless and support me. When my husband and I were expecting our third baby, I went into pre-term labor at twenty-eight weeks. Thankfully, my doctor was able to stop it, but I was on strict bedrest for the next two months. I wasn't even able to sit up to eat or drink and could only get out of bed to use the bathroom. So, what did our church community do? Well, they loved us well and took great care of us, and I literally had to lay there and take it. People volunteered to come over to take care of our two little girls. People signed up for weekly cleaning responsibilities. People made supper, watered flowers, grocery shopped. Our small group even held weekly meetings in our bedroom. It was a time of my life where I was overwhelmed. Overwhelmed by God's love being poured out on me through His people.

This community taught me practicing hospitality and living in community are strongly intertwined. So much so that for me, it's hard to separate the two, and I've found I must be intentional about both. I must be willing to open my heart, my home, and/or my ears. I must be the one to invest because no one can do it for me. I've learned that I do have a place, a part to play. And just like hospitality and community are closely knitted together, so also is the giving and receiving.

Jamie McKenzie *is married to her best friend, has a bunch of kids, and loves to garden.*

Winter

If we had no winter, the spring would not be so pleasant: if we did not sometimes taste of adversity, prosperity would not be so welcomed.

Anne Bradstreet in *Meditations Divine and Moral*

HOSPITALITY PLANS

Winter days are always weird for my soul. They're short in terms of daylight but long in the time it seems to take the sun to shine again. One winter recently was especially wet, and it wasn't the pretty white wetness. Instead, there was so much rain that people joked about building arks and floating away in their backyards. Our country road flooded multiple times that winter. Then at the beginning of March we got a peek into spring. The sun stayed for multiple days in a row, mornings required jackets but afternoons warmed everyone's days, and sandals were appropriate attire. About that same time, I started in on plans—for the coming-soon days as well as summer. I registered my kids each for a camp or two. And I scheduled our pool opening.

I realize plans aren't the solid ground on which we build our lives, but they help me navigate a busy season I want to enjoy. Of course, planning is something my first-born girl understands. I would say I instilled that quality in her, but really, I'm pretty sure she was born with it.

One morning as I was frantically making breakfasts and packing lunches, my then-seven-year-old daughter said she thought the notepad hanging on the refrigerator would be a good place to list what she wants me to get from the grocery. Well, hello, independent planning. She wins for being the first member of my family to want to invest in the grocery list. So she wrote down "bagles" and "cream chees"—I told you, she was seven. We had finished what we had of those two items that morning and she figured they needed to be replaced.

I honestly didn't think about the list as I went about my day because I wasn't meal planning or grocery shopping that day. I figured I'd consult the list another day after more things had been added. When Cate got home from school that afternoon, she wanted to talk about the list.

"So did you get the bagels and cream cheese? You know I want the white cream cheese and not the pink one?"

"Yes, I know you like the plain better than strawberry. But I haven't been to the grocery store yet."

She seemed disappointed in me. "But we're out of those things," she said.

I started to explain instant gratification—and why we don't need to live like that. Bagels and cream cheese don't require a special trip to the grocery. They're on the list. I'll get them when I'm there next. Planning requires some waiting and anticipation—such a life lesson, especially for a first-grader.

I think I was fairly convincing. She seemed to understand. It wasn't long before she added other things to the list. And then I caught myself doing the same thing—with Amazon, because, hello, epitome of (nearly) instant gratification with Prime shipping. I was out of light bulbs—added them to the cart. I needed a certain size battery—check. Talk about convenience of necessary (or maybe sometimes unnecessary) items showing up at my door.

I suppose instant gratification doesn't matter much when it comes to batteries and light bulbs or even bagels and cream cheese. But I've learned some of my most profound lessons of trusting God when I had to wait.

I waited to get pregnant, never actually did, and learned God heard the desires of my heart as He built our family through adoption, which, of course, required more waiting.

I've waited for the phone to ring or mail to arrive.

I've waited for a friend to understand or my husband and me to get on the same page.

Honestly, I don't usually wait patiently. I want to rush the silence and uncertainty. Other times I assume I've got it all figured out and don't need to wait on anyone or The One who actually is in control.

Psalm 46:10 says, "Be still, and know I am God." I've heard this verse often, but it's only been as a 40-year-old woman that I've really started to understand it. In this verse, "still" actually means "cease striving."[19] Being still in the presence of God is more than just not moving; it's actually about our mental posture and being willing to surrender our stubborn wills.

I eventually bought a bag of blueberry bagels and whipped cream cheese, not the strawberry flavor. The batteries and light bulbs arrived on my doorstep forty-eight hours later. God led us to adoption three times after He made it clear we were supposed to stop trying to conceive. My phone rang. Necessary conversations happened in the right time.

But even as we wait for whatever is next, we can invite others into our lives. We don't have to wait until we're finished with college or married or finally a mom to welcome people to our lives. Sure, hospitality plans. But sometimes planning may just mean you're committed to being open to whatever God has for you in this moment and the moments to come. Maybe planning means we decide to be still so we can remember who is actually in control. And when we're still, we're more likely to see a need or be ready for a meaningful conversation.

Of course, in this culture of instant gratification, time is a funny concept. Now, my teenage girl likes to shop for trendy clothes and fairy lights to decorate her bedroom walls, brought Crocs back to her wardrobe, and wears holey jeans. She's lost all her baby teeth, navigated more than two years in braces, and spends time fixing her beautiful hair. Like all of us, she's learning the hard way that waiting makes us better, eventually. Yes, she can Amazon Prime something if she has a gift card left over from her birthday or Christmas, but she's also required to wait on green lights from her parents. I pray she knows our boundaries and restrictions are because we believe our heavenly Father honors waiting, even if our culture stinks at doing so.

I believe God has this whole world, including my girl, in His hands. Sometimes He makes it clear what we should do, where we should go, and when the changes should happen. Other times we have to wait. But we can worship and live and serve and rest and learn while we wait because God's got a plan—and because our names are scribbled on the notepad in heaven that's much more permanent than the one on my fridge. And that seems like a good plan.

STORY OF SHARED LIFE
MEGAN THOMAS

I believe we were created to know and love God. By learning more about God, His desires and His nature, I can use that knowledge to love Him more. I think this is true about people too. The more I know someone, the better I can love and serve them.

But how do we come to know, like really know, others? I've learned, the most meaningful relationships I've had with others have been built in each others' homes—playing a game, sharing a meal, studying scripture, lingering over coffee. This is why hospitality matters. By inviting others into our homes, we are inviting them to be known. We are saying, I want to know you and by knowing you, love you.

I am a coffee drinker. I drink about three cups a day—two in the morning and one during my children's nap time. I do not care what flavor or brand. I am happy with gas station coffee or a cup from our local, trendy coffee shop. I buy the bulk size Folgers because it is usually the cheapest.

During the school year, a friend usually stops by my house one morning a week. Our oldest children are in school and our younger ones play together while we can chat over coffee. Whenever she comes over, I make her a cup of Kona Brand coffee from Kroger. Kona Brand is her favorite. I know this because this is what she makes in her home. I make it because I want her to know she is wanted here, she's known and loved here. I want her to come in and feel wanted lingering over a cup of coffee, or two.

When I think of someone who is hospitable, I think of my friend Lori, who hosts a Bible study for women in her home each Thursday evening. When you enter her home, the room you enter is lined with chairs. They don't really match and they are squeezed in so that she can fit as many chairs as possible. The wall is filled with scripture, encouraging phrases, and pictures of her friends. You can tell that in Lori's mind, this room isn't her room but her friends' room.

One of her chairs is hideous. It's big, has old floral fabric, and adds no aesthetic value to that room. When I asked her about that chair she said, "Oh, that's Miss Molly's chair. I can't stand that chair, but Miss Molly loves it so I have kept it." Miss Molly is an older woman who comes to Lori's Bible study. Lori wants Miss Molly to come, and not just come but come and feel welcomed, wanted, and known.

Hospitality plans in the smallest ways because it prepares for specific people to come.

Megan Thomas *is a wife and mom of four who loves community.*

Hospitality Entertains

We plan our winter social life around the Murray State basketball schedule. We meet friends for dinner before the home games in our small town. We have friends who travel with us to a few away games —sometimes in a 14-passenger van we borrow or more recently taking up every seat of my eight-seater Pacifica. We have favorite restaurants in Clarksville, Tennessee, and Evansville, Indiana, and on the way to Cape Girardeau, Missouri, and Martin, Tennessee that are pit stops before we head to an away game to root on our Racers.

I know sports aren't everyone's form of entertainment, but Greg and I both would choose a college basketball game over an art museum, a college football game before a musical, and a Major League Baseball game instead of any sort of dance recital. We both grew up watching sports, so it naturally became something we did together.

We have season tickets to Murray State basketball and football games. We try to go to a St. Louis Cardinals baseball game most seasons. We also like University of Kentucky football and basketball, and occasionally make our way to Lexington for a game. Then we had kids—and we kept doing it.

But the Racers are our favorites. And it's good common ground for local socializing.

I have pictures of Cate and Ben sleeping at MSU basketball games. Of course, my third-born child is way too worried she'll miss something to close her eyes at a game. Although like her siblings, R-A-C-E-R-S is among the first words Rachel could spell. (It probably helps it's so much like her own name!) Even as a toddler, Rachel recognized the mascot and the logo around town.

Cate is old enough to have memories of players she's loved watching. As Ben started loving to play basketball, he also asked more questions about the rules and strategies. We know where friends sit in the arena and more people know where we sit because my husband often stands up and starts cheers. During televised games, I get texts when people see Greg standing and cheering on their televisions.

With sports come stories of perseverance, achievement, and sometimes loss. In a culture where everyone thinks they deserve a participation trophy, it's good for the kids to see the world keeps turning after your team loses. And, of course, it's fun to celebrate with teams we've come to know from our seats.

When Cate was four, I knew my girl had a crush on a Murray State basketball player when she worked him into conversation while grocery shopping. While in Kroger's frozen food aisle, she said, "We are in row 11, like Donte Poole's number."

I assured her she was right. And I smiled inside. Celebrity crushes are harmless and cute, right? She noticed when his name was mentioned during basketball games and liked to watch him score. She was overwhelmed with emotion when he was named MVP at the conference tournament. She cringed when he hurt his nose during the first of two NCAA games. She didn't understand why he had to graduate and play his last game in a Racer uniform. And she'd be insulted if you didn't know the name Donte Poole.

Cate was a nervous wreck the first time she met him. She actually could have met him a couple weeks earlier when we happened to see him, but she hid behind Daddy's leg instead. (I get it! Remember, I did the same thing when I was young!) She basically stopped near him long enough for me to take a picture, gave him a five, and mumbled "Hi," and then wouldn't stop talking about meeting him. A full-blown crush, I tell you. Why else would a girl talk about a boy while her mom looks at frozen vegetables and Texas toast?

We won't forget the 2011-12 season, when my girl had her first crush and fell in love with basketball while the Racers were national media darlings with their 31-2 record. Around that same time, Cate's preschool sent home a note saying some Racer players were coming to play with the kids after this historical season. She was ready to meet Donte—again. She talked about it so much that her two-year-old brother Ben was saying, "Meet Donte!"

Cate was more prepared to meet her crush a second time. She wrote him a note and included a picture of him playing basketball. I knew it was him playing in the picture because she wrote "11" over him.

Donte,

> *You are my favorite Racer. I like to watch you play.*
> *Love,*
> *Cate Taylor*

I remember watching her give him the note. And I remember watching him listen to all her many words. I have no idea what she said. She probably remembers, but even if she doesn't, this is why I document things. We'll tell her about it all over again when she's grown up, probably with some other crush who makes her daddy and me nervous.

The Racers made national fame again in the 2018-19 season when guard Ja Morant went from nobody outside Dalzell, South Carolina, and Murray, Kentucky, knowing his name to being one of the most-talked-about NBA draft picks. In fact, he was the second pick in the 2019 NBA draft. He had a fabulous rookie season (even if it was cut short because of the coronavirus epidemic) and so many kids, especially in Racer Nation, wear his #12 jersey. Yes, including my son. That's what he got as a birthday present for his tenth birthday, just before his own elementary school basketball season began. There's a Ja fan club at most practices with an assortment of jerseys in Murray State blue and gold, Grizzles' navy and light blue, or throw-back Grizzles' teal.

Our kids have benefitted in other ways from us being a sports-fan family. Basketball games give me a chance to say yes, introduce my kids to other towns, and let go of our bedtime routine. Naturally, I'm a rule follower who wants everyone to follow my rules, but I've had opportunities to give the kids treats and grace. Those things don't come naturally to me, so being a sports fan has helped me keep perspective on life and offer some hospitality to my kids and friends.

Yes, we'll be watching as many games as possible in March, so come join us on our couch in front of the TV. There's always room for more.

STORY OF SHARED LIFE
CORBITT POLK

Hospitality is my sweet spot! I love entertaining and spending time with others. As a couple, my husband, Rod, and I have never shied away from throwing the class party with outdoor movie night, inviting over our entire small group for dinner, or entertaining more than fifty people at our first Friendsgiving. I've been asked, "How could you handle this?" and people say, "I would be terrified!" It just boils down to we love God and we love people.

For us, hospitality is relational. The Lord loves us and in turn, we love others. We really find a common ground with each person to start from. It can be something as simple as parents and kids that go to school together, your neighbors, church friends, or your family.

We have two girls, who are now eleven and thirteen. When they were younger and starting at new school, I took it on as my personal mission to get to know all the kids my child would be socializing with!

One fall of first grade, we decided to invite all of my younger daughter's class over for an outdoor movie night. We had previously been invited to an outdoor movie night and came straight home and ordered our own inflatable movie screen! We recognized immediately the chance for fellowship and community with others. We practiced a few times on a smaller neighborhood scale then jumped into a bigger gathering with the classmates and their parents. Name tags were required! We had people bring blankets and chairs. We provided the movie, lemonade, and s'mores. Most of the class came. Most parents stayed for the evening; a few dropped their kids off. We had a great night. We met a lot of people that we didn't know and that started the school year off great! We are still friends with those we met for the first time that night.

A few years ago, we moved to Greenville, South Carolina, after living in central and western Kentucky all of our lives. Talk about going from knowing all kinds of people to not knowing anyone. We soon discovered being strangers isn't who we are. December rolled around and our new neighborhood had a Facebook page. My neighbor posted she would love to throw a gingerbread party for the neighborhood kids. She mentioned that she would get everything needed for the party, including preparing the gingerbread houses and getting all the icing and sprinkles. But she needed one thing: a place to have it. Yes, I volunteered our house! We had only been there five months and we were going to host our first event! I was so excited. When I told my husband, he was not so excited. He asked, "You did what?"

We were off to the races. We had other neighbors bring snacks. All we had to do was host. It was quite the event! We had more than sixty parents and children. The children's ages ranged from one to fifteen years old. We had icing and sprinkles everywhere! Do you know what else we had? Laughter, community, and new memories. All because we said yes. Other moms couldn't believe I was calm and not freaking out about all the mess. I guess for me the good definitely outweighs the bad. One mom said, "There is no way I would do this at my house."

Homes are built for making messes and memories and for living fully. For us, living fully is sharing life with others.

Corbitt Polk *lives in Nicholasville, Kentucky, and enjoys serving the Lord and her two daughters. Her husband passed away in June 2020, about two years after being diagnosed with cancer.*

HOSPITALITY INVESTS

After having watched basketball her whole little life, Cate and two of her friends decided to play on their school team the winter she was in seventh grade. Remembering my own middle school days, I was proud my girl who shies away from the spotlight wanted to play a new sport that would involve being on a court in front of an audience while competing against other teams who would be more skilled than our school's young team. I basically considered her wanting to play a win. And that was before she learned how to play forward, grab rebounds, and even put back some of her teammates' misses.

Turns out the Lady Lions, which spanned fourth through eighth grades at our small school, won a couple games that first season. They got beat by 30 points multiple other times, but each game gave the girls more confidence, which showed up in their willingness to take more shots and in their behavior and conversations away from the court. Being part of a team taught my girl rules to a sport that has long been part of our social life, but, more importantly, gave her a new sense of community. She belonged with her friends in a deeper way because they chose to be brave and try something new together. She invested in a shared activity and not only bettered her skills but also her community.

The Lady Lions represented our sweet, small school community. Since kindergarten, Cate has attended this classical, Christian school that's steadily grown to have about one hundred kids in almost all the grades from preschool through high school. Having extracurricular activities like basketball, archery, and running club has created a greater sense of community among not only the students but also their parents. Other students have made signs to cheer on their classmates. Teachers have come to watch games and volunteered to coach cheerleading, teach volleyball, and organize opportunities when they could be at home. Hospitality invests beyond the paycheck like that.

Some of the friends I see the most in this parenting season are other parents from my big kids' school. We chat at pickups, sit next to each other at games, carpool to field trips, and bring treats to the same classroom parties. We invest in our kids' lives but come away with a deeper community too. So then we also make plans to see each other in the summer when our lives aren't revolving around the school calendar, celebrating birthdays together and confiding in one another when we're having hard days.

Investing in friendships with like-minded moms has helped me navigate motherhood. Sometimes this is a weary job! But raising kids is a worthwhile investment that takes time over the course of lots of seasons. Galatians 6:9 is a good reminder for me: "And let us not grow weary of doing good, for in due season we will reap, if we do not give up."

I've heard this before, but it struck me in a new way when I was stretched among three parenting seasons. These words reminded me that with each conversation, boundary, ride home from school, and correction, I'm investing in my kids and the life we're building together for God's glory. Having friends in similar parenting seasons, as well as ones a few steps ahead of me, reminds me all the mental energy we're investing is worth it.

More recently, parenting has involved conversations about cell phones, sleepovers, and vacations; discipline regarding grades and attitudes; and training and establishing habits. Yes, you can play basketball; no, you can't have a cell phone. Yes, you can go over to her house after school, but you can't spend the night.

I've talked with like-minded friends, many of whose kids are my kids' classmates, and discussed with my husband, who thankfully lives on the same page with these things. Articles have affirmed why my kids won't have cell phones anytime soon and why we don't do sleepovers, but they've also reminded me living counter-culturally is hard but not beyond where God has called us, especially if we bring others with us.

My others have come as I befriended my kids' friends' parents, but also through engaging in shared activities with others. I have a group of fellow writer friends who first gathered online and then at my lake house for a retreat. We talk and text on Voxer almost every day. We came together initially to share each other's writing and products, but we ended up praying together through lots of hard situations, discussing various parenting seasons, sifting through theological questions we didn't always agree upon, and sharing details of our daily lives. We still root each other on in our craft, but we also consider each other dear friends.

I also have a group of Bible study girls. We sat down at the same table as part of a larger group, but as we studied scripture together, we shared pieces of our lives. We've had playdates at the park with our young kids and gathered at my pool when Bible study is on summer break. A few of those girls were among the first people with whom I shared my complicated grief when my dad died. Delana could be our mom and loves to cook for us. We sent gift cards to Leslie when she miscarried a baby and to Tara when she was sick. We prayed for kids and decisions and families. We recommend books to each other and check in on each other when we've gone too many days without touching base.

These groups of friends began on specific common ground and have continued to be a foundation in my life because we went beyond that initial reason for gathering. Maybe it's not writing or studying the Bible. It could be any hobby or interest that brings you together with others you may not have otherwise known.

One sunny, winter afternoon while Rachel was stealing a nap in the Kroger parking lot, I revisited Galatians 6:9-10, this time in The Message: "So let's not allow ourselves to get fatigued doing good. At the right time we will harvest a good crop if we don't give up, or quit. Right now, therefore, every time we get the chance, let us work for the benefit of all, starting with the people closest to us in the community of faith." I thought about my community of fellow moms, writers, and Bible study mates. I remembered God's faithfulness in my everyday life regardless of the season and recommitted myself to investing in my kids and my friends.

STORY OF SHARED LIFE
ANGELA TAYLOR

Charles and I met our first day of Introduction to Music Theory class at Murray State, and there were instant sparks. He was funny, charming, and attractive, and apparently he felt the same way about me. We were married ten months later and have now been married for a little more than twenty years. We are both middle children, and we were the first in both of our families (and in our set of friends) to get married, have children, and (out of most of our age group) have our own home. Basically, we hit all our major milestones pretty early on compared to those who we associated with, and that changed things for us drastically. It was something that we never anticipated.

We used to have large groups of friends over every week, and frequently got invitations to "hang out." We'd play ultimate Frisbee, run to the movies, or eat impromptu meals with friends, and we just thrived at being the social butterflies that we were. That continued after marriage. However, after our first child Elijah's birth, and our out-of-state move so Charles to work on his veterinarian doctorate, we saw a big drop-off. We didn't really get invited anywhere. Charles was busy with school and part-time jobs, and I was busy with our babies. (Ethne came along soon after Elijah.) Life was busy, but at times lonely.

These are the things that most folks don't talk about—the shift that comes with marriage and child-rearing. You still have friends, but it's rare that you can truly invest time in one another like you did in the past. You're too busy trying to keep tiny people alive and pay the bills. Once we were living again in our hometown, back with our childhood friends, and back with our families, the invitations still did not come. Everyone was busy. Eventually, we had created a brood of seven beautiful children. You can imagine, with that many children, we had been in "survival mode" for years. It wasn't until recently, when more of our children were independent and could actually be helpful, that we realized that we had failed miserably at teaching our children about "hospitality."

The Bible has so many verses about hospitality, and I know one that I've heard on repeat over the years has been Hebrews 13:2: "Do not neglect to show hospitality to strangers, for thereby some have entertained angels unawares." It doesn't give exceptions. Show hospitality except for if you have more kids than you can manage . . . or unless you have a stressful job . . . or insert whatever you find cumbersome. It simply states that we are to show hospitality.

Charles and I felt convicted. That's when we decided to invest in our friends instead of waiting on the sidelines. Even if the invites were never reciprocated, we were going to make the effort to invest in other people.

So, what does that mean to a family of nine? How on earth have we invested? We have dedicated at least one evening a month, sometimes more, to having another family over for dinner and fun. Sometimes that includes karaoke parties, game nights, street-hockey, or just good conversation. Charles and I have dedicated at least one lunch per month to a friend. We each meet up separately with a friend to reconnect and have adult conversation. We both have purposefully started using texts, calls, emails, and social media to stay connected with those that we cannot meet face-to-face as often as we'd like. We purposefully check in. We've become more active in the global church and not just our small congregation. We attend family retreats, VBSs, revivals, singings, and the like to connect to other Christians. Lastly, we stay involved with our community and give to things that benefit not only our friends but acquaintances and strangers. We've actually made new friends through our community service.

(Keep in mind that these are ideas that have worked for our family, but hospitality and investing can and will look different for yours.)

Charles and I have come to the conclusion that a person will always accomplish whatever they prioritize and put their energy into. We know that a family with seven children can seem overwhelming and a bit daunting, and not everyone has the means or the facilities to accommodate such a mass of bodies. Instead of expecting hospitality at every turn, we've become determined to not only invest in our community but in our children by trying to model what hospitality should be. We want them to have that sense of community and family, not just with us, but with many others. As Christians, hospitality is just one tool in our toolbox of showing kindness and edifying one another.

Angela Taylor is a follower of Christ, the wife of a preacher and entrepreneur, the mother of seven children (with the eighth expected in January 2021), a lover of fairytales, and a graduate of Murray State University.

HOSPITALITY HELPS

Click List became a fast friend.

I got the flu a few days before Christmas 2017. That meant I missed out on a few gatherings with relatives and friends I had been looking forward to seeing while we were visiting my mom. I rested on her couch and shared Tamiflu with my husband, but I really wanted my own bed so we came home a little earlier than we had planned.

And that meant we needed more food than I had planned.

Obviously, going to Kroger wasn't a good idea but trying out the new online order service at my local grocery story was the perfect solution. From an app on my iPhone while I sat in the passenger seat of my minivan, I ordered milk, eggs, bacon, crackers, cheese, chicken nuggets, and whatever else my family told me they wanted. Then my husband showed up at the agreed upon time the next morning and brought home sacks full of groceries while I tried not to share my germs with anyone.

I may have been coughing, but at least my family could eat. Hospitality is about serving those in your own house, even if you aren't your best self.

I used Click List again the next week because it was still Christmas break. Then I used it again the next week because I had a third free pickup. And then I used it again after being at home for four straight days—just think of all the meals we consumed during that time—because ice and snow in Kentucky doesn't get cleared from the roads quickly and more snow was forecasted.

By the way, my husband graciously picked up those groceries between snows in his four-wheel drive vehicle. The world definitely slows down around here when it snows, but some people, like my husband and the Kroger employees, still showed up to work, thankfully.

I didn't leave my house that January until Snow Day No. 8, and only thanks to my friend Makenzie. We thought we were going to get out—and my kids even started shoveling the ice from around my tires. Even when I was able to move my van for the first time all week, my tires wouldn't get any traction on my road. Then I got stuck in my driveway trying to turn around and maneuvered only enough to get my van out of the actual road.

I was truly grateful Makenzie understood the isolation I felt when I thought I was getting out and then couldn't. She extended hospitality to me when she went out of her way to bless me with my first outing in more than a week. Of course, my kids were happy to get out and have some pizza for lunch too.

(All of this was a few years before the socially distanced life we lived during the coronavirus epidemic that shut down most everything and kept us home for many, many more days than those snow days. I'm guessing my perspective would have been different had I known a longer, harder season of isolation was coming our way in 2020.)

Around that same time, when my kids were 10, 8 and 2, I found myself stuck in another way, more emotionally and spiritually. I was mentally still reeling from some changes from previous years. I had poured out everything I had relationally and not positioned myself to let God refill me. I was trying to navigate the tension between my first-born, perfectionist-leaning ways and my son who is all middle child and was diagnosed with ADHD earlier in the year. Plus, childhood junk crept into my present ordinary days.

I ended up making a call to schedule my first-ever counseling session. The ongoing conversations with my counselor were one avenue God has used to restore my soul. In that counseling room, the words bounced back and forth from all the goodness in my life to how I always see room for improvement. I felt brave for doing this hard work.

The counselor and I addressed the reality of my parenting season: tween girl emotions, elementary boy behavior, and toddler shenanigans. We talked about stress and worked on a shift in perspective that accepts reality and makes time—even in small pockets throughout the day—to regroup. We talked about how I am the opposite of ADHD and am equipped to teach my son the routines and time management skills he needs. Also, my boy is in a position to help me enjoy ordinary life. My counselor Ashley reminded me I am meant to be Cate's mom, Ben's mom, and Rachel's mom.

At the same time, I spent some time learning about the Enneagram personality types. Knowing my type and where I go in seasons of stress and of health has been eye-opening for me. I know experts would caution against doing so, but I also typed my son. It's been a good lesson in recognizing that my stress-filled words hurt him and make him shut down, realizing when I'm my best self I'm adventurous like he is, and knowing all our different personality tendencies are connected.

None of this is exactly news, but it was freeing for me, who has always outwardly processed life, to sit for an hour and do so with a third party. Of course, sometimes I can't just sit and process all the deep feelings of life and have to instead grocery shop with all three kids because that's real life. Just take the one day I got in the Express Lane. I'm pretty sure both big kids started counting the items in our cart as soon as they realized it was the shorter conveyor belt.

Ben, who was eight and a typical middle child who recognized rules but didn't always choose to follow them, said, "Mom, you can't go in that checkout lane because it says 15 items and we have 16."

"It says about 15, so we're good," I offered as I started loading the apple juice onto the conveyor belt while simultaneously trying to keep toddler Rachel from choosing all the candy bars and gift cards she could reach. Perhaps he needed a lesson on estimation and rounding when I could focus a little better. With all her first-born ways, Cate tried to define "about" for Ben again and let me know we did indeed have more than 15 items. She's obviously all about the rules. I just kept loading the items while they continued discussing and I made sure none of us sneaked a Snickers.

Most importantly, while I navigated life during counseling

sessions and in the Kroger aisles, I recognized we don't have to bring the pieces of ourselves to God polished and put together. Asking questions and accepting help is therapeutic. God will take all the broken parts to make something beautiful and sweet.

STORY OF SHARED LIFE
COURTNEY FRENCH

For a lot of my adult life, I have struggled with how to minister to others. I am a homeschooling mom and also work a few hours a week as a nurse—so the audience I am around most days is not very large. I don't really have a circle of people that I am around on a regular basis as mine seems to change often. I don't really fit in with the moms who work full-time outside of the home, nor do I seem to totally fit in with the moms who are at home full-time. I sometimes long for a group or circle that is "my people," but I am realizing that's not where God has me. He puts me in different circles at different times and, honestly, that has frustrated me sometimes.

My husband owns his own business and is constantly talking to people in the community. He has shared with me countless stories of people he has been able to talk to about the Gospel or minister to in some way. I have struggled at times through the years feeling like the things I am doing are not "big" enough or "important" enough. Even though I'm so thankful he has had those interactions, at times I have felt envious of the work he is doing and wished God had me in a different role.

During those times, God is so kind to remind me that He has me where I am for a purpose. He gently reminds me that the people I am serving matter, regardless of how many. I don't have to have a particular "group" or "circle" for Him to use me. He can and will use me no matter where I am and no matter how big the audience may be. Jesus quietly, humbly washed the feet of those who were around Him, not on a stage or in front of a huge crowd. He did a job they could have done themselves, but He did it out of the great love He had for them. He gave us an example of humility and how to serve.

I love this quote by Mother Teresa so much I put it in my living room: "Do small things with great love." It is a good reminder to me that even the smallest things matter.

As believers, we are all part of the body of Christ, and each have a role—none more important than the other, but each necessary in order to function properly. This can be hard to accept at times because sometimes others' roles look much more appealing or important.

Each part is important. Just as I should not look down on or be envious of someone else's part, I should also value and find contentment with the part God has given me. My role is important, no matter how big or small it may seem. He has put me in this place for a purpose.

My days can vary so much. Some weeks I am home a lot and others not so much, so ministry for me can change almost daily! Some days ministering to others looks like reading a devotional with my kids or having patience when I help them through a hard math lesson or school project. Sometimes I sit with my daughter when she isn't feeling her best and just needs someone to listen or help my son get ready for an overnight basketball trip.

Other days I care for an elderly person in the hospital by getting them ice water or help them get their room organized so they can reach their belongings better. Some days I take a meal to someone who has been sick or had surgery or spend time with a single mom or friend who is struggling in her marriage. Sometimes I send flowers or a book to a friend to try to brighten their day or make soup for my grandparents to put in their freezer. Some days ministry is babysitting for a friend or sitting with someone while their loved one is in surgery. And yet other times I restock the supplies at our church or clean.

Recently God put on my heart to start a monthly women's ministry at our church to connect women in my community. Doing so scares me, but I'm thankful for a different opportunity to serve.

We have so many different ways to minister to others! They may not seem big to me, but they matter to the person who is on the receiving end. I want to look around at the people God has placed in my life at this time and ask myself: How can I wash their feet? How can I serve them? May He give us all eyes to see who He has in our lives right now to help.178

Courtney French *is a wife, mom of two, and a nurse whose favorite things include the beach, running, books, and dogs.*

HOSPITALITY CONTINUES

My family was about a year into a card-playing tradition with four other families when I recognized the significance. It was an accidental tradition. Megan invited my and Courtney's families over to eat grilled cheese and play Nertz. And then Tiffany and her family came over too. Then another time Brandy and her family joined us. We ended up gathering about once a month. We played at my house a couple of times that first year, but more often at Megan's.

Community started in the kitchen and then overflowed into the dining room and living room and backyard. Hospitality does that, starting one place and continuing into other rooms, onto the next gathering, and through other parts of life. Our husbands and kids all knew each other too, and their conversations sometimes drifted to business. The big girls played with the little girls, while the boy contingent in the middle ran in and out the door, through mud sometimes, and always on a competitive mission.

Nertz involves each person or couple having their own deck of cards because people play in piles in the middle and then cards are separated at the end of each round for scoring. We started joking about how we needed our own decks of cards with our pictures on them. Right in time for our year anniversary of this accidental tradition, I ordered five decks of cards, one for each couple with personalized pictures. I had them for several weeks and was thrilled when I got to surprise my friends with them at my dining room table.

Midway through the first year of playing Nertz with these friends is when my dad died. I pulled away from making as many social plans as I had in the past because I was buried in grief. Yes, I love playing games and want to win, but, more importantly, this group was life-giving then and still is. Their laughter and sharing stories while we eat then sit (or, um, stand) and toss cards around the table are gifts.

These Nertz games are just one social tradition in our lives. I can mentally think through the year and know there are some standing gatherings that sustain me. It reminds me of a passage from *When You Find Another*, a book filled with friendship stories: "The loveliest friendships of all feed our souls with the sweet and beneficial conversations they provide. They encourage us and push us forward to be all God created us to be. They comfort us and restore our souls when we feel broken, wounded or weary. They make us laugh and bring us joy. They remind us of who we are and whose we are and why we are who we are. And they give us faith and courage to keep on going."[20]

Perhaps it's my quality time love language, my Enneagram One ways that loves a plan, or my human desire to belong, but I love anticipating traditions. And, really, something I love happening just a couple of times makes me want to claim it as tradition.

In March, or sometime around then, we join our best friends for a trivia night fundraiser that benefits a story time program another friend leads. When our kids were younger, that story time was a favorite weekly tradition. Now, supporting it by participating in a fun event remains a worthwhile tradition. In the seven years of participating, our team has acquired matching T-shirts that say "Friends who trivia together stay together," four wins, and a second-place finish after a tie-breaker.

In May, portions of my extended family often gather at our vacation rental on Kentucky Lake to spend Memorial Day weekend together. For a long weekend in the summer, married friends who I introduced to each other two decades ago come visit us. Their oldest of three boys shares the same name as my Ben and the whole crew now shares memories of childhood summers.

At the end of each summer, right before school starts, we host a swim party and potluck for our kids' school's board members, teachers, and staff. I love how this recurring activity bonds people beyond the classroom.

In November, we have a Friendsgiving meal with three other families. It started with a bigger group of friends from church and morphed into what it is today as people moved around.

These traditions and so many other gatherings are how hospitality continues weaving itself throughout our lives and years. With that, I do have to remember sometimes traditions change, but hospitality can still continue, even when we're unsure of what's next.

As many traditions grew and changed and morphed into new traditions, God taught me about seasons and the value in rhythm. Too often my response to a new season is holding on too tightly, trying to replicate previous seasons. God has made each season beautiful and appropriate in its own time. Yes, spring, summer, fall, and winter repeat, but each winter looks different than the one before because God is transforming me. I'm not the same this year as I was as a child or even just last year. There can be similarities and traditions from one year to the next, but the details change from one season to the next, from one year to the next. That's both wonderful and terrifying.

At the end of what was a hard year, when a favorite season didn't look familiar because grief interrupted, I wasn't sure of much when I looked at everything happening in the world, but I knew I'd been transformed, again, for the better.

Nothing in this life stays the same. That almost seems like a threat, but really it's a promise too. Traditions anchor us, but our God won't leave us where we were in the winter by the time springs starts blooming new life.

CONTRIBUTORS

I couldn't imagine writing a book about hospitality without a little help from my friends. I hope you loved their stories like I love sharing real life with them. Learn more about them here.

Hospitality Begins
Katie Kerns is a wife, mom of two boys, and a teacher. She loves God, her family and friends, iced coffee, singing Disney songs, petting dogs, and hugging.

Hospitality Teaches
Kayla Slack is a wife, mama of two, and home health nurse who finds joy in Jesus and her life with her family. Find her at www.instagram.com/flameandfinesse, where she shares how she stays healthy, her life with her cute kids and husband, and choices to choose joy over fear.

Hospitality Heals
Sarah Goodrich lives in Frankfort, Kentucky, with her husband and four children.

Hospitality Adventures
Amanda Conquers is a cop's wife, mom to four, and an anxiety-struggler learning to be an overcomer. She shares real-life stories and resources to help others overcome on her website amandaconquers.com and on Instagram at @amanda_conquers.

Hospitality Celebrates
Amanda Pennington met her husband, Payton Pennington, at Murray Christian Fellowship, which she shares about in her story. Even though they enjoy traveling and visiting friends from MCF

who have moved away, they know God has called them to keep their home in Murray, Kentucky.

Hospitality Nourishes

Ashlee Young is wife to Jeff, a stay-at-home mommy to Leela, and likes adventures, tea, and a good book.

Hospitality Ministers

Katie Cunningham is a pastor's wife who works in her home raising three sons and a daughter. She and her husband, Kory, host a podcast called "This House," where they share about marriage, family, parenting, church, and how it all relates to the gospel. Katie also moderates the live Q&A sessions for Hardin Baptist Church at www.facebook.com/hardinbaptistchurch.

Hospitality Interrupts

Shelly Divido is wife to Harry, mother to Hannah, missionary and founder of Light of the World Ministries, but, most importantly, a daughter to the King of Kings. Learn more about her family's ministry and life in Guatemala at www.facebook.com/LOTW. Ministries.

Hospitality Befriends

Shelley Sapp is a stay-at-home mother of four currently living near Colorado Springs, Colorado. At the time of publication, her family is opening a shop to sell homemade ice cream and encourage sweet gatherings. Discover more about Shelley and her new business at www.facebook.com/lolleysicecream.

Hospitality Shares

Mary Jost is a Jesus-loving Georgian who loves hiking with her family, traveling to Disney World, and going to concerts.

Hospitality Lingers

Emilie Reinhardt is the definition of an ESFP and an enneagram 7, through and through. The chief end of Emilie is to go to bed tired, every night, because then life was lived to the absolute fullest. Constantly figuring out what mountain to hike next, or death-defying stunt to pull off, life doesn't beat her down, even with spinal reconstruction surgery, thirty-one screws and a couple titanium rods. There's still a lot of life to be had, it just may not look quite the same as the first thirty years of her life. On any given day you can find her in the woods, on a mountain, playing with one of her dogs, babysitting one of her hooligans (niece or nephew), or galloping around on her horse.

Hospitality Connects

Christen Price is a speaker, author of "Invited: Life a Life of Connection, not Perfection" and helps leaders lead with courage and compassion. But those are her official titles. At home, you'll find her with her best friend and husband, Raleigh, as they parent their four crazy kiddos – twin girls Adeline and Maralee and boys Ridley and Raleigh James. They live in Alabama. Connect with her at christenprice.com or @christenpricestudio.

Hospitality Grieves

Leslie Cates is a happy wife, a worship leader, and a coffee-loving stay-at-home mom raising three kids she was blessed with through the miracle of adoption. She shares recipes, homemaking stories, and marriage and motherhood memoirs at thecozylittlekitchen.blogspot.com.

Hospitality Serves

Katie Mitchell lives in southern Indiana with her husband, Aaron, who she met through the author, and their boys, Ben, Will, and Wes; works as an oncology/hematology nurse practitioner; and is known for her laugh and her "best-ever" recommendations.

Hospitality Welcomes

Jaclyn Tompkins is the daughter of the King, wife, momma of three, and teacher of many.

Hospitality Supports

Mary Carver is a writer, speaker, and podcaster who loves finding (and sharing) Truth in unexpected places. Find her at marycarver.com.

Hospitality Loves

Jamie McKenzie is married to her best friend, has a bunch of kids, and loves to garden.

Hospitality Plans

Megan Thomas is a wife and mom of four who loves community. She lives in Murray, Kentucky.

Hospitality Entertains

Corbitt Polk lives in Nicholasville, Kentucky, and enjoys serving the Lord and her two daughters. Her husband passed away in June 2020, about two years after being diagnosed with cancer.

Hospitality Invests

Angela Taylor is a follower of Christ, the wife of a preacher and entrepreneur, the mother of seven children, a lover of fairytales, and a graduate of Murray State University. At the time of publication, she and her husband are expecting their eighth child in January 2021.

Hospitality Helps

Courtney French is a wife, mom of two, and a nurse whose favorite things include the beach, running, books, and dogs.

HOSPITALITY ACKNOWLEDGES

Greg, I'm glad we do so many things in this life together, but I'm okay never grocery shopping together. You're my best friend and after all these years I think you're getting pretty close to being able to read my mind.

Katie Kerns, I'll forever be grateful we got to be neighbors and always wish that could happen again. Until then, I'm thankful you'll always feel like home to me.

Jaclyn Tompkins, we've been to more than 130 places together, but I'll always be most thankful for the real-life meals, games, and walks in all the seasons we've shared. I truly don't know what I'd do without you.

Sarah Goodrich, I still miss you living in Murray, but I'm grateful you remain in my everyday life. I wish neither of us experienced the grief we did in May 2019, but I don't know how I would have survived that summer or so many of the days since without your understanding being a text away.

Courtney French, you've known me basically the whole time I've been a mom, and I'm better for it. Our friendship has looked different in various parenting seasons, but I'm thankful we can always pick up where we left off. And Greg and I are always going to take the credit for making you into a basketball fan!

The Gachokas, we love basketball season with y'all, but we really love getting to be your friends. We've shared so many van and bus rides, meals, and conversations that have been made us feel like the real winners.

Megan Thomas, thank you for inviting me into your house each week in the summer of 2019. I said yes to that weekly commitment before I had any idea how much I'd need to gather with that group and learn more about God's promises. I'm grateful for every conversation we've had about parenting and faith, the opportunities to taste your superb grilled cheese, and all the Nertz games we've played.

Kroger employees, thank you for being friendly and accommodating. We've gotten free candy bars and balloons while grocery shopping, help navigating the aisles during multiple renovations, no judgement when I dropped a six-pack of IBC Cream Soda, and more stickers than I could count in a lot of toddler years for three kids. Plus, your Click List employees are happy and efficient.

The Best Ones, I will always make food for you guys when we gather together. You feed my soul in so many ways, encouraged me to write this book and helped me brainstorm a title for it, and, most importantly, are more than just the "writer friends" label I use to describe you to anyone else in my life. Amanda Conquers, the way you find beauty in everyday moments and then share with us is a gift. Anna Rendell, the way you celebrate seasons, holidays, and others encourages me. Christen Price, you invite others in so beautifully. Erika Dawson, your words and products speak so much truth into my life. Kayse Pratt, bringing us together as a group is one of the greatest hospitality blessings in my life. Mary Carver, your friendship and editing skills make me a better person and writer.

Precept table girls, sitting with you every other Thursday morning is among my very favorite places to be. Ashlee Young, your sweet, wise ways encourage me. Delana McCuiston, the food you make us every time blesses my soul. Katie Cunningham, thanks for leading us, always having a book or podcast recommendation for me, being a like-minded friend, and welcoming me to my bonus church. Lauren Holt, your ability to be real and welcoming in the same moment is a gift. Leslie Hack, thanks for letting us into your hard season and always showing up with a smile. Monica Bidwell, thank you for inviting me to this group in 2015 and being faithful to keep our families connected. Tara Ladd, I'm glad we sat down at the same table and connected quickly.

⤳ABOUT THE AUTHOR

Kristin Hill Taylor believes in seeking God as the author of every story and loves swapping these stories with friends on her porch. She lives in Murray, Kentucky, with her husband and three kids.

With her family of mostly extroverts, she can often be found hosting people at her house in the country, watching sporting events or having game nights with friends, or answering her kids' questions about whether anyone is coming over for dinner.

Her first self-published book *Peace in the Process: How Adoption Built My Faith & My Family* is the story of God's faithfulness through a season of infertility, three adoption processes, and the days since. Through it all, Taylor learned God hears the desires of our hearts, wants us to live in community, and uses all of our circumstances for our good and His glory. The book includes contributions from other adoptive moms, her children's birth moms, and resources for families who want to grow through adoption and the people who support them.

She has a bachelor's degree in print journalism from Murray State University and worked in various newsrooms before she became a stay-at-home mom. Join her at her virtual porch at kristinhilltaylor.com.

facebook.com/khtwriter

twitter.com/kristinhtaylor

instagram.com/kristinhtaylor

ALSO BY
KRISTIN HILL TAYLOR

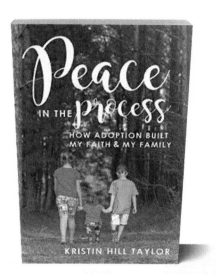

PEACE IN THE PROCESS

Peace in the Process: How Adoption Built My Faith & My Family is the story of God's faithfulness through a season of infertility, three adoption processes, and the days since. Through it all, Kristin Hill Taylor learned God hears the desires of our hearts, wants us to live in community, and uses all of our circumstances for our good and His glory.

This book includes contributions from other adoptive moms, the Taylor children's birth moms, and resources for families who want to grow through adoption and the people who support them.

Learn more about the book, read a sample chapter, listen to a playlist, and download adoption resources at kristinhilltaylor.com/peace-in-the-process. The book also is available at Amazon.

SOURCES

[1] Baker, Lisa-Jo. *Never Unfriended: The Secret to Finding & Keeping Lasting Friendships.* B&H Books, 2017.

[2] Lucado, Max. *Outlive Your Life: You Were Made to Make A Difference.* First Edition, Thomas Nelson, 2010.

[3] *Blue Letter Bible.* www.blueletterbible.org. Accessed March 18, 2020.

[4] Baker, Lisa-Jo. *Never Unfriended: The Secret to Finding & Keeping Lasting Friendships.* B&H Books, 2017.

[5] Thompson, John W., and Randy Scruggs. *Sanctuary.* Whole Armor Publishing Company, 1982.

[6] *Blue Letter Bible.* www.blueletterbible.org. Accessed March 12, 2020.

[7] Martin, Shannan. *The Ministry of Ordinary Places: Waking Up to God's Goodness Around You.* Thomas Nelson, 2018.

[8] Gaines, Joanna. "A Look at Risk." *Magnolia Journal*, no. 15, summer 2020.

[9] Alcorn, Randy. *In Light of Eternity: Perspectives on Heaven.* 1st ed., WaterBrook, 1999.

[10] Niequist, Shauna. *Present Over Perfect: Leaving Behind Frantic for a Simpler, More Soulful Way of Living.* First printing June 2016, Zondervan, 2016.

[11] Adams, Julie Porter. "The Heart of Why We Gather." *Magnolia Journal*, no. 15, summer 2020.

[12] Lee, Jennifer Dukes. *The Happiness Dare: Pursuing Your Heart's Deepest, Holiest, and Most Vulnerable Desire.* Tyndale Momentum, 2016.

[13] Strong, Kristen. *Back Roads to Belonging.* Revell, 2019.

[14] Oxford University Press (OUP). "Connection." *Lexico.Com*, www.lexico.com/en/definition/connection. Accessed 8 June 2020.

[15] Tripp, Paul David. *New Morning Mercies: A Daily Gospel Devotional.* Crossway, 2014.

[16] Gerth, Holley. *You're Made for a God-Sized Dream: Opening the Door to All God Has for You*. Revell, 2013.

[17] Exodus 17:8-16 NIV.

[18] Piper, John. "Strategic Hospitality." *Desiring God*, 18 Mar. 2020, www.desiringgod.org/messages/strategic-hospitality.

[19] *Blue Letter Bible*. www.blueletterbible.org. Accessed March 5, 2020.

[20] Harms, Kay. *When You Find Another: A Conversation About Friendship...Among Friends*. Lulu.com, 2017.

Made in the USA
Middletown, DE
01 September 2020